Trade Policy, New (

The WTO, FTAs and Asia Ri

Trade Policy, New Century

The WTO, FTAs and Asia Rising

RAZEEN SALLY

The Institute of Economic Affairs

First published in Great Britain in 2008 by
The Institute of Economic Affairs
2 Lord North Street
Westminster
London SW1P 3LB
in association with Profile Books Ltd

The mission of the Institute of Economic Affairs is to improve public understanding of the fundamental institutions of a free society, by analysing and expounding the role of markets in solving economic and social problems.

A CIP catalogue record for this book is available from the British Library.

ISBN 978 0 255 36544 4

Many IEA publications are translated into languages other than English or are reprinted. Permission to translate or to reprint should be sought from the Director General at the address above.

Typeset in Stone by MacGuru Ltd
info@macguru.org.uk

Printed and bound in Great Britain by Bell & Bain Ltd

CONTENTS

About the IEA   228

THE AUTHOR

Razeen Sally is co-Director of the European Centre for International Political Economy (ECIPE), a new international economic policy think tank based in Brussels. He is presently on leave of absence from the London School of Economics and Political Science (LSE), where he has taught since 1993. He received his PhD from the LSE in 1992, and did post-doctoral research at INSEAD in France. He is Senior Research Associate at the South African Institute of International Affairs in Johannesburg. He has been a Visiting Professor at the Institut d'Etudes Politiques (Sciences Po) in Paris, Senior Visiting Research Fellow at the Institute of Southeast Asian Studies in Singapore, a Visiting Fellow at the University of Hong Kong and the Australian National University, and Director, Trade Policy, at the Commonwealth Business Council in London. He is on the Academic Advisory Council of the Institute of Economic Affairs in London, and on the Advisory Board of the Cato Centre for Trade Policy Studies in Washington, DC.

FOREWORD

Any trade economist aiming to address a wider readership faces challenges. One is to break free from the thickets of mind-numbing jargon and technical detail that infest the subject. Another is to explain lucidly why a liberal trade order, founded on the counter-intuitive principle that nations gain far more from freeing imports than from expanding exports, matters to the world. This monograph succeeds admirably on both counts, while setting out a radical new policy agenda.

The author's premise is that, 60 years after the establishment of the multilateral rules-based system, international trade policy has lost its way. The six-year-old Doha trade round is struggling and seems destined to produce only a modest outcome – if it does not peter out completely. The World Trade Organization (WTO) is increasingly hamstrung by a cumbersome negotiating model, politicisation of its deliberations and indulgence of civil society critics hostile to free markets. Around the world, protectionist rumblings are growing louder.

Meanwhile, even governments once unequivocally committed to multilateralism are rushing headlong into bilateralism and regionalism, in the name of speeding liberalisation. Yet, as the author points out, this explosion of so-called free-trade deals will do little to remove existing barriers, and risks instead creating new ones. Too often, politically driven initiatives that lack hard commercial logic or substance threaten to fragment the global economy into a patchwork of discriminatory rules and regulations that distort or impede trade.

The author's solution is a return to basics, inspired by the precepts of Smith and Hume. Liberalisation, he argues, will regain impetus only if governments wrest primacy over trade policy from global institutions, whose 'top down' approach has yielded diminishing returns. The priority should be unilateral liberalisation, with China's autonomous opening-up as its most inspiring example. But the paper also emphasises that removing external barriers is not enough to enhance economic performance: it must be buttressed by reforms that strengthen the rule of law, promote sound institutions and transparency, guard against anti-competitive practices, and otherwise improve economic efficiency. In sum, governments should start treating trade policy less as a matter for diplomatic negotiation and more as a central element of domestic economic policy.

That necessarily implies a diminished role for the WTO – an outcome which, the paper argues, is in any case preordained by the organisation's serious structural deficiencies. The author calls for a less ambitious post-Doha WTO agenda, focused more on strengthening trading rules than on expanding market access, and for big decisions to be entrusted to self-selecting groups of countries rather than involving fully the entire membership, much of which participates little in global trade.

Of all the risks confronting the free trade order, perhaps the greatest is complacency. More than half a century of trade liberalisation has bestowed huge cumulative economic benefits on the world. But its success has also caused those achievements to be taken increasingly for granted – all the more so because the global economy has recently proved so remarkably resilient in the face of repeated shocks. There are signs of 'reform fatigue' in many countries, while constraints on government intervention in the market appear to be growing looser. As the fate of the Doha Round illustrates, 'political will' and the leadership needed to bulldoze domestic obstacles to liberalisation are in short supply.

This paper is a refreshing antidote to such inertia. As well as making a robust theoretical and empirical case for the benefits of free trade, it provides a penetrating analysis of the dangers confronting it. It also sets out practical prescriptions for getting trade policy back on the rails. It is confident in its judgements – and unsparing in its condemnation of those whom the author perceives to be enemies of liberalism. Informative, well argued and, above all, highly readable, it is a stimulating contribution to the emerging debate on where trade policy should go in the post-Doha world.

GUY DE JONQUIÈRES
former World Trade Editor
Financial Times

The views expressed in this monograph are, as in all IEA publications, those of the authors and not those of the Institute (which has no corporate view), its managing trustees, Academic Advisory Council members or senior staff.

ACKNOWLEDGEMENTS

I should like to express my gratitude to the Earhart Foundation in the USA for a grant to write this book. Then there are those who have influenced, inspired and encouraged me along the way. My thanks in particular to David Henderson, Deepak Lal, Nancy Upham, Peter Draper, Chandra Athukorala and Fredrik Erixon. Lastly, my thanks to Jonas Pettersson and Erik van der Marel for super-efficient assistance.

SUMMARY

- Ideas about free trade started in the West and were originally exported to the rest of the world. But, today, the major challenges for trade policy come from Asia.
- Trade is still the engine of prosperity and the handmaiden of peace. The 'New Globalisers' that have been freeing trade have seen rapid economic growth, reductions in poverty and improvements in welfare.
- The authentic case for free trade should be set in the context of classical liberal political economy and, as such, Western political opinion needs to move on from considering the promotion of free trade as a top-down process driven by supranational institutions. Instead it should see free trade as an integral part of a domestic liberal political agenda.
- Supranational organisations, including the World Trade Organization (WTO), have become too unwieldy to be effective in promoting radical trade reform; they should focus on ensuring that their rules are implemented effectively rather than on seeking radical liberalisation.
- Protectionist interests are alive and well and have influence both within individual countries, such as the USA, and within supranational organisations.
- The relatively liberal Western democracies should focus their trade policy on removing remaining explicit protectionist

barriers but, perhaps more importantly, also on simplifying and making more transparent inhibitions to trade such as rules of origin and anti-dumping provisions. It is also important that a 'culture of evaluation' develops in the West so that implicit barriers to trade are properly scrutinised – especially within the EU.

- Slower reformers, generally lower-income countries, should focus on lowering tariff barriers and quotas – they generally lack the governance capacity to implement more complex reforms. Less developed countries need to lower their tariff barriers between themselves.

- There are over 180 Preferential Trade Agreements (PTAs) in force. PTAs are spreading like wildfire throughout Asia. In practice, many tend to be 'trade light' tools of foreign policy and diplomacy.

- Those Asian countries that have successfully integrated into the world economy have done so through unilateral liberalisation. China has reduced its tariffs from an average of 65 per cent twenty years ago to 10 per cent today. This process of unilateral liberalisation must continue, but the USA and the EU need to ensure that the right background for liberalisation exists by eliminating protectionist rhetoric and actions, such as so-called 'anti-dumping' measures.

- A classical liberal, 'small-government' domestic culture, which includes the promotion of unilateral free trade, will help ensure that the development of free trade is not knocked off course by vested interests. Dangerous vested interests include those promoting protectionism in the name of environmentalism, protecting strategic industries or promoting domestic security.

- The USA is an indispensable anchor for maintaining global peace. Its leadership is currently unchallenged. It has a particularly important role in engaging constructively with Asian countries to ensure that the best political climate exists for the continued development of free trade and internal liberal reform in Asia.

TABLES AND FIGURES

GLOSSARY

ACP	African, Caribbean and Pacific countries
AFTA	ASEAN Free Trade Area
ANZCERTA	Australia–New Zealand Closer Economic Relations Trade Agreement
APEC	Asia-Pacific Economic Cooperation
ASEAN	Association of South-East Asian Nations
COMESA	Common Market of Eastern and Southern Africa
CU	Customs Union
EPA	Economic Partnership Agreement
FDI	Foreign Direct Investment
FTA	Free Trade Agreement
FTAAP	Free Trade Area of the Asia Pacific
GATS	General Agreement on Trade in Services
GATT	General Agreement on Tariffs and Trade
IMF	International Monetary Fund
MERCOSUR	Mercato del Sur
MFN	Most Favoured Nation
MNE	Multinational Enterprise
NAFTA	North American Free Trade Agreement
NBER	National Bureau of Economic Research
NGO	Non-Governmental Organisation
NTB	Non-Tariff Barrier

OECD	Organisation for Economic Cooperation and Development
LDC	Less Developed Countries
PTA	Preferential Trade Agreement
ROO	Rules of Origin
SACU	South African Customs Union
SAFTA	South Asian Free Trade Area
S&D	Special and Differential Treatment
SPS	Sanitary and Phytosanitary Standards
TBT	Technical Barriers to Trade
TRIMS	Trade Related Investment Measures
TRIPS	Trade Related Intellectual Property Rights
WTO	World Trade Organization

Trade Policy, New Century

The WTO, FTAs and Asia Rising

1 A SHORT INTRODUCTION

Not that the story need be long, but it will take a long while to make it short.

HENRY DAVID THOREAU

Western influence on the world, though still great, is declining. Eventually our societies will be the minor partner in the terrestrial enterprise. What do we want the majority to believe about the liberal idea that animated the West's historical achievement and that we continue to profess, but have, in recent decades, ceased to act upon? What kind of world will it be, if the majority comes to believe that the idea is a sham?

JAN TUMLIR

This is a little book on a large subject: trade policy in the early 21st century. It has two objectives. The first, in the spirit of Thoreau's quote above, is to Keep It Short. My intention is not to write another bulky tome on the World Trade Organization (WTO), Free Trade Agreements (FTAs) and other aspects of trade policy. Rather it is to capture big trends, sum them up concisely, and communicate directly and engagingly to a broad audience of interested readers.

The second objective is to give my account a non-Western, especially Asian, slant – hence the headline quote from Jan

Tumlir, who was for long the director of research at the General Agreement on Tariffs and Trade (GATT) and its informal in-house philosopher. The classic themes of trade policy, revolving around free trade and protectionism, originated in the West and have been framed by the West for the rest of the world. But the major challenges facing trade policy today come increasingly from outside the West, and particularly from a rising Asia. The 21st century, so we are told, is the Asian century.

Now for a little background to give a sense of this book's 'mental atmosphere' – one of George Orwell's favourite terms. My last book, *Classical Liberalism and International Economic Order*, is an intellectual history of free trade versus protection, as seen in the classical-liberal tradition from David Hume and Adam Smith to F. A. Hayek. The grand, universal themes addressed in that big book frame the picture for this little one. What is the relevance of free trade (or freer trade) today? What is its role in modern globalisation? What are the existing and emerging protectionist threats, ideological and material, to open commerce across national borders? Why is it important to counter them? How can a freer-trade agenda be put into practice in the years and decades ahead?

In this first decade of the new century, I have worked mostly on current trade-policy issues: the WTO and its Doha Round; FTAs, especially in Asia; and other trade-policy developments in China, India and South-East Asia. This has been a mix of academic and think-tank writing, consultancy projects and opinion pieces for newspapers. Through such variety I have come to think of myself less as a 'normal' academic and more as what Ralf Dahrendorf calls a 'straddler' – someone at the junction of academic research, policy and opinion formation. I hope my straddling has been seasoned by the truly empirical experience of work and travel across Asia in particular.

Hence, as a straddler, I lay this book before interested and intelligent readers: practitioners keen to rise above day-to-day events and policy minutiae; academic experts with a practical bent and an interest in the real world; and general readers simply concerned about the issues covered. This book is *not* intended for the over-specialised nerd.

Finally, here is the batting order for the chapters that follow. Chapter 2 provides a potted intellectual history of the debates on free trade and protection, from classical antiquity to the late twentieth century. It is intended to shed light on the big trade-policy questions of today and tomorrow.

Chapter 3 covers the political economy of trade policy. It looks at the state of play in trade policies, especially across the developing world. Then it examines the driving forces of trade-policy reform: crises, interest groups, ideas, institutions and factor endowments. Then follows a section on trade policy on different tracks: unilateral measures, the WTO, FTAs, and the role of foreign aid. Finally, it sets a broad agenda for further liberalisation and associated structural reforms – in a difficult political climate in which scepticism about liberalisation and globalisation has been on the rise.

Chapter 4 is about the WTO. It covers the transition from the GATT to the WTO, and then developments in the Doha Round. It defends a framework of multilateral trade rules, but makes the case for more realism and modesty in a post-Doha WTO. That demands a shift in the focus of WTO business, and changes to WTO decision-making. The USA and China will have to lead necessary changes if the WTO is to retain relevance and avoid marginalisation.

Chapter 5 discusses preferential trade agreements (PTAs). Its focus is on the recent proliferation of PTAs in Asia, which is playing catch-up with the rest of the world. Nearly all PTAs are 'trade light' and of little commercial value. They do not threaten to break up the global trading system, as happened in the 1930s, but they are not vehicles of genuine regional and global economic integration. Furthermore, PTAs are storing up political and economic complications.

Chapter 6 makes the case for unilateral liberalisation in the 21st century, arguably more important as a liberalisation vehicle than the WTO or PTAs. China is now the engine of unilateral liberalisation in Asia and beyond; and it is vital that this engine does not sputter and stall. That depends on a combination of internal and external political and economic conditions.

Chapter 7 – the concluding chapter – looks ahead to the next few decades. It makes the case for free trade in the new century. It highlights emerging issues that will come to dominate trade policy, and looks at the role of governance at national and global levels. It argues that free trade should fold back into a Smithian classical-liberal framework. The case for free trade should again be made as part of a package of individual freedom, limited government, free markets and unilateral liberalisation. That, however, cannot be realised in a vacuum: it depends on a stable international political order. That in turn depends on constructive US leadership, good bilateral relations between the USA and other powers, and realistic, workable multilateral institutions.

2 FREE TRADE VERSUS PROTECTION

The doctrine of free trade, however widely rejected in the world of policy, holds its own in the sphere of the intellect.

FRANK TAUSSIG

All theory is grey, my friend, but green is life's glad golden tree.

GOETHE, *FAUST*, PART TWO

The two quotes above signal the polar extremes in the debates for and against free trade. Since Adam Smith, classical and neoclassical economists have proclaimed the superiority of free trade in theory. The American economist Frank Graham called it 'a ubiquitous and timeless principle'. To Stanley Jevons it was 'a fundamental axiom of political economy'. At the other end of the spectrum, implacable opponents of free trade, from counter-Enlightenment Romantics such as Carlyle and Ruskin to today's anti-globalisation postmodernists, reject it on anti-economic grounds. It is a product of the 'dismal science' and the 'quackery' of economists, as Carlyle put it. It is a bloodless laboratory experiment, they say; a Utopia grafted on to the human skin, with damaging social consequences.

The free-trade-versus-protection debate is not as Manichaean as the views above suggest. The reality, of course, has shades of grey in between. This chapter tries to get a sense of where thinking on the issue stands today. It does so via a potted history of ideas. The controversies swirling around free trade and protection are first traced back to their roots in classical antiquity and brought forward to the Middle Ages. There is then a section on mercantilism pre-Adam Smith. After that comes the emergence and establishment of free-trade doctrine in classical political economy, especially in the writings of Adam Smith and David Hume. Then follow nineteenth- and twentieth-century developments.

The purpose of this roundabout method is to avoid a shallow repetition of current – and mostly ahistorical – arguments for and against free trade. Intellectual history, hopefully, will give us a wider, but also less superficial, panorama of this central debate in early 21st-century globalisation.

From classical antiquity to the Middle Ages[1]

Political, philosophical, ethical and legal arguments for and against free trade have existed since ancient Greek and Roman times. But these are all non- or meta-economic arguments. Economic analysis – the systematic observation and interpretation of how economic phenomena interact – came much, much later in the mercantilist tradition.

The leading and oldest non-economic argument in favour of free trade – namely that it leads to international peace – probably originated in an early Christian 'universal economy' tradition. It had a cosmopolitan outlook and welcomed unfettered trade

---

1   This section draws on Jacob Viner's brilliant Wabash lectures. These wonderful miniatures are found in Jacob Viner, *Essays on the Intellectual History of Economics*, ed. Douglas A. Irwin, Princeton University Press, Princeton, NJ, 1991, pp. 39–81. Also see Douglas A. Irwin, *Against the Tide: An Intellectual History of Free Trade*, Princeton University Press, Princeton, NJ, 1996, ch. 1.

across the seas as a means of bringing about better contact, under-standing and friendship among peoples, eventually leading to the universal brotherhood of man. This was seen as a sign of benefi-cent divine intervention. In the Middle Ages, natural-law theo-rists, from Vittoria and Suarez to Grotius and Pufendorf, regarded free trade as part of the *jus gentium*, the law of nations. The eighteenth- and nineteenth-century classical liberals, along with Immanuel Kant, made an explicit connection between free trade and international peace. Richard Cobden was perhaps the most powerful advocate of free trade as the central means of ensuring peaceful international relations. That idea was carried forward in the thinking of Woodrow Wilson and Cordell Hull. The latter, arguably, was the spiritual father of the post-1945 multilateral trading system. As he declared, 'unhampered trade dovetails with peace; high tariffs, trade barriers and unfair economic competi-tion with war ... I will never falter in my belief that enduring peace and the welfare of nations are indissolubly connected with friend-liness, fairness, equality and the maximum practicable degree of freedom in international trade'.[2]

Protectionist arguments – again overwhelmingly non-economic – were probably more influential down the ages. Plato and Aristotle embodied a Greek political-philosophical tradition that denigrated economic activity as something for social inferiors, especially women and slaves. Politics was the superior, virtuous activity, the preserve of male citizens in the *polis*. The latter was supposed to be politically self-contained, for which it had to be economically self-sufficient, save for trading in necessities. That meant minimal contact with foreigners.

---

2   Cordell Hull, 'The true nature of trade', *The Memoirs of Cordell Hull*, Macmillan, New York, 1948, p. 81.

Finally, much Christian thought over the centuries had an anti-economic streak, with a bias against foreign trade. The latter supposedly inflames the vices of worldliness and avarice. It pulls people away from the religious life, which is intimately bound up with ascetic virtues.

Mercantilism[3]

Mercantilist thinking dominated in the two centuries before Adam Smith's publication of *The Wealth of Nations*. Economic analysis emerged slowly and imperceptibly during this period, though Schumpeter says that mercantilism was essentially 'pre-analytic': its proponents were mostly pamphleteers full of assertions, opinions and axes to grind; they were not dispassionate analysts.

Mercantilism's political context was the ascendancy of the Westphalian system of nation-states. Kings and princes were in the business of nation-building. They projected their power within their states by centralising control over domestic societies and economies; and projected their power externally in warlike international relations, not least to grab or defend overseas territory. In the economic sphere, the self-interested, profit-seeking merchant, and wealth creation more generally, were increasingly welcomed – a radical departure from antecedent attitudes. But it was considered folly to leave merchants to their own devices. Rather the state had to ensure that self-interested behaviour was guided, deliberately and forcefully, so that it served national interests. It was

---

3   This section draws on Irwin, op. cit.., ch. 2; Jacob Viner, 'Mercantilist thought', in his *Essays on the Intellectual History of Economics*, op. cit.., pp. 262–76; Joseph A. Schumpeter, *History of Economic Analysis*, Routledge, London, 1950, pp. 335–78.

incumbent on the state to make trade flow in the 'right' channels while avoiding the 'wrong' channels. Hence, notwithstanding a ragbag of diverse and often conflicting views within the mercantilist canon, its organising principle was *raison d'état.*

Mercantilism had at least five main planks: the accumulation of specie; a favourable balance of trade; promotion of infant industries; the belief in an international zero-sum game; and the preservation of domestic stability.

First, some mercantilist writers sought to accumulate specie (gold in particular) in the national exchequer through maximising exports and minimising imports. They considered a hoard of specie to be a leading indicator of national wealth. It was also 'the sinews of war', a repository of funds to pay mercenaries and fight wars. The accumulation-of-specie argument is now considered outdated, even by modern-day mercantilists.

Second, many (perhaps most) mercantilists advocated a healthy trade surplus by means of export promotion and import protection – mercantilism's 'two great engines', according to Adam Smith. Many considered this to be the leading indicator of national wealth. As Thomas Mun, a leading English mercantilist, put it: 'The ordinary means therefore to encrease our wealth and treasure is by Forraign Trade, wherein wee must ever observe this rule; to sell more to strangers yearly than wee consume of theirs in value.'[4]

Thus intervention in foreign trade, through customs duties, bounties, quotas, foreign exchange controls and outright bans, was to complement a panoply of internal controls on production and consumption.

---

4   Quoted in Lionel Robbins, *A History of Economic Thought: The LSE Lectures*, ed. Steven Medema and Warren Samuels, Princeton University Press, Princeton, NJ, p. 52.

Third, from Elizabethan times onwards, mercantilists favoured the promotion and protection of infant industries to kick-start industrialisation. Manufacturing was considered a superior wealth generator to agriculture and other forms of economic activity.

Fourth, mercantilists generally believed in Hobbesian international politics and economics. One nation could only gain at the expense of other nations, since international wealth was finite.

Fifth, domestic social stability was a mercantilist imperative. Foreign trade had to be controlled precisely because, if left uncontrolled, it would disrupt the domestic social balance.

'Mainstream' economists, from David Hume and Adam Smith to Eli Hecksher and Jacob Viner, have gone out of their way to dismiss mercantilism's central planks as economic nonsense. A trade surplus (or deficit), in isolation, does not tell us anything: and it is certainly not a good indicator of national wealth. Manufacturing is not intrinsically superior to other forms of economic activity. And international trade, if governed by market forces, is a positive-sum game that delivers all-round gains. Hence Paul Krugman's dismissal of mercantilist shibboleths as 'pop internationalism'. To David Henderson, this is 'do-it-yourself economics'. Nevertheless, with the exception of the archaic accumulation-of-specie argument, the main tenets of pre-Adam Smith mercantilism endured into the nineteenth and twentieth centuries, and are alive and well today. They retain powerful ideological appeal.

The emergence of free-trade doctrine[5]

The *economic* defence of free trade, as opposed to its defence from

---

5   This section draws on Irwin, op. cit., chs 3 and 4.

non-economic standpoints, only got going in the eighteenth century. In the interstices of mercantilism, several writers had insightful flashes of the benefits of an unrestricted international division of labour, with, at its core, the interdependence of self-adjusting imports and exports, and of trade and payments. Some came close to saying that free trade, not protection, delivers a superior gain in terms of national wealth creation. Charles Davenant expressed this position pithily: 'Trade is in its nature free, finds its own channel, and best directs its own course: and all laws to give it rules and direction, and to limit and circumscribe it, may serve the particular ends of private men, but are seldom advantageous to the public.'[6]

This turned the mercantilist presumption – that the state should direct trade into 'good' and not 'bad' channels – on its head. It set up the principle of non-intervention in trade, akin to the French Physiocrats' governing principle of laissez-faire.

Now it is time for Adam Smith to enter the scene. His genius was not originality; rather it was to draw on a range of thought before him, seasoned with acute observation of history and the world around him, to come up with a sweeping *synthesis* of the economic system and its interrelated parts. The result was his *Inquiry into the Nature and Causes of the Wealth of Nations*. He drew particularly on preceding economic analysis (from the Physiocrats, for example) and his own Scottish-English tradition of moral philosophy.

The governing principle of the Smithian economic system is 'natural liberty' (or non-intervention), which allows 'every man to pursue his own interest his own way, upon the liberal plan of

---

6   Quoted in ibid., p. 54.

equality, liberty and justice'. And, as Smith went on to say, 'All systems of preference or restraint, therefore, being thus completely taken away, the obvious and simple system of natural liberty establishes itself of its own accord.'[7] Thus self-interest (broadly conceived), if left to its own devices, is conducive to the public good, particularly by maximising the wealth of the nation. The crucial qualification is that this is not a vision of anarcho-capitalism or unadulterated laissez-faire. Rather it depends fundamentally on an appropriate framework of rules ('justice' in Smith's terminology), which the state is charged with instituting, updating and enforcing.

Smith extended this economic system animated by natural liberty from the domestic to the international sphere, from intra-national to international trade. Book IV of *The Wealth of Nations* laid out a comprehensive system of international trade, with a many-sided defence of free trade that remains unsurpassed. Smith's contemporary and close friend David Hume wrote some brilliant sketches on international trade,[8] but it was Smith who furnished the overarching system.

Free trade in Smith and Hume: an elaboration[9]

By the end of the eighteenth century, free trade had become the

---

7   Adam Smith, *An Inquiry into the Nature and Causes of the Wealth of Nations*, ed. Edwin Cannan, University of Chicago Press, Chicago, IL, 1976 (1776), p. 208.

8   See David Hume, *Writings on Economics*, ed. Eugene Rotwein, University of Wisconsin Press, Madison, 1970 (1758).

9   This section draws especially on Razeen Sally, *Classical Liberalism and International Economic Order: Studies in Theory and Intellectual History*, Routledge, London, 1998, ch. 3. Also see Irwin, op. cit., ch. 5; Robbins, op. cit., lectures 11–16; Schumpeter, op. cit., pp. 181–94; Viner, 'Adam Smith and *Laissez Faire*' (ch. 2), 'Adam Smith' (ch. 10), in his *Essays on the Intellectual History of Economics*, op. cit.

established presumption in Scottish-English political economy. British policy at the time, however, was still largely protectionist; and the consensus outside Britain still favoured protection over free trade. Let us now probe deeper into the classical-liberal system of free trade in Hume and Smith.

Both Hume and Smith made a full-frontal attack on mercantilism as their point of departure. Hume's attack was directed at the accumulation-of-specie argument, which he considered self-defeating given automatically adjusting movements of trade and payments. Smith attacked 'real-economy' distortions caused by import protection and export promotion in the pursuit of a trade surplus. Both Scotsmen reserved some of their most vivid language to excoriate mercantilism's dog-eat-dog, zero-sum view of international trade. Here is a sampling from Hume:

> Nothing is more unusual, among states which have made
> some advances in commerce, than to look on the progress
> of their neighbours with a suspicious eye, to consider
> all trading states as their rivals, and to suppose that it is
> impossible for any of them to flourish, but at their expense.
> In opposition to this narrow and malignant opinion, I will
> venture to assert, that the increase of riches and commerce
> in any one nation, instead of hurting, commonly promotes
> the riches and commerce of all its neighbours.[10]

And here is Smith in similar vein:

> By such maxims as these, however, nations have been
> taught that their interest consisted in beggaring all their
> neighbours. Each nation has been made to look with an
> invidious eye upon the prosperity of all the other nations
> with which it trades, and to consider their gain as its own

---

10   David Hume, 'Of the jealousy of trade', in Hume, op. cit., pp. 78, 82.

loss. Commerce, which ought naturally to be, among
nations, as among individuals, a bond of union and
friendship, has become the most fertile source of discord
and animosity.[11]

Hume and Smith: economic analysis

Smith grasped the insight that moving from protection to free
(or freer) trade generates a one-shot efficiency gain: imports
replace costlier domestic production, thereby releasing domestic
resources for more productive uses, including exports. He then
dismissed various protectionist arguments as a wasteful diversion
of resources. His analysis was based on absolute cost advantages.
What he failed to grasp was the essential insight of comparative advantage, later established by Torrens and Ricardo. This
holds that the gains from trade spring from comparative costs
(comparing costs of producing a good *within* one country as
opposed to comparing absolute costs *between* countries): imports
can replace domestic production even if they are more expensive
to produce in absolute terms. Comparative advantage, the foundation of international-trade theory from Ricardo onwards, points to
wider and deeper specialisation, and all-round gains from trade,
while absolute advantage points to more partial specialisation and
partial gains from trade.

That said, Hume and Smith were much more concerned with
a dynamic, rather than a static, view of international trade. To
them, the dynamic gains from trade are critical to the long-run
progress of commercial society – far more important than short-
term resource-allocation effects.

---

11   Smith, op. cit., p. 519.

Hume's main observation on the dynamic gains from trade relates to what we now call 'technology transfer'. He viewed unfettered international trade as a conveyor belt for the transmission of ideas and technology across borders. This allows individuals and enterprises within nations to spot and then imitate better practice abroad, leading to improvements in their own performance, and, in the aggregate, to overall economic growth. To Hume, this is a process of mutually beneficial competitive emulation among nations, akin to competition in economic markets. As Hume said, 'A noble emulation is the source of every excellence.'

Smith's major insight was that international trade widens the geographical extent of the market. This allows a deepening of the division of labour (i.e. more specialisation), which enables enterprises to reap economies of scale and increase productivity. This in turn feeds into economic growth. Today this is known as the 'increasing returns' argument.

Both Hume and Smith – Smith in particular – stressed the role of institutions in linking openness to the world economy and economic growth. The gradual improvement of domestic institutions is the lynchpin of the system. Opening to the world economy creates new incentives to firm up 'hard' and 'soft' infrastructure (to use modern terms). For example, traders link farmers and other small-scale producers in the hinterland to coastal ports, whence their goods are exported. Then come roads, railways, the telegraph and other forms of transport and communications. Competition from abroad and awareness of international trading possibilities create the demand to improve property rights, contract enforcement, and other forms of regulation and (what we now call) governance. Such institutions help to maximise the gains from trade and associated foreign investment. Over time, this interaction between institutions and external openness leads to capital accumulation, investment, entrepreneurship and the diversification of a growing economy. Such was Smith's vision of development. His was a model of an open-ended, dynamic, institution-rich economy. Its assumptions were realistic – a far cry from the perfect-competition, general-equilibrium, institution-free comparative-advantage models that held sway in the nineteenth and twentieth centuries.[12]

Hume and Smith: political economy

Hume and Smith – again, Smith in particular – fortified their economic defence of free trade with explicitly political arguments that highlighted the dangers of protectionism in practice. Three arguments stand out.

First, there is what we now call the 'rent-seeking' or 'government-failure' argument. To Smith, protectionism issues directly from the struggle of organised interests within the state. Producers organise for collective action; they lobby and capture government in order to protect their supernormal profits from being competed away by more efficient domestic and foreign rivals. In excoriating language, Smith referred to 'the clamorous importunity of partial interests', which, 'like an overgrown standing army … have become formidable to the government, and upon many occasions intimidate the legislature'. And further: 'Thus are the sneaking

---

12   See Hla Myint's brilliant essays on Adam Smith's theory of external trade and its link to development. Hla Myint, 'The "classical theory" of international trade and the underdeveloped countries', *Economic Journal*, LXVIII(270), June 1958; Hla Myint, 'Adam Smith's theory of international trade in the perspective of economic development', *Economica*, 44, 1977.

arts of underling tradesmen erected into the political maxims for the conduct of a great empire.'[13]

Hence, to Smith, protectionism is neither a passing, cyclical phenomenon, nor primarily the result of zero-sum interstate competition. Rather it is a structural feature of domestic politics that spills over into international economic and political conflict.

Second, Smith saw free trade in *constitutional*, not just superficially political, terms. Apart from being an economic-efficiency device, it is an instrument of domestic constitutional refurbishment. Protectionism is inherently arbitrary and opaque: it is all about back-room deals between producer interests, politicians and bureaucrats – at the expense of the public good. Free trade, by limiting such activity, brings an element of fairness and transparency to politics and government. Above all, free trade is non-discriminatory in the procedural sense. Protectionism fixes the results of the competitive game, thereby discriminating between persons. In contrast, under free trade, outcomes emerge from the competitive game itself, buttressed by the equal (i.e. non-discriminatory) treatment of persons before the law. This is central to Smith's notions of the rule of law and justice.

Third, Smith pondered the pros and cons of unilateralism versus reciprocity. Should governments liberalise trade unilaterally, i.e. independently of the trade policies of other governments? Or should they liberalise reciprocally, i.e. only if others do likewise? On balance, Smith came down in favour of unilateral free trade, more on practical political grounds than through hard economic reasoning. Reciprocity involves incessant haggling between governments; it is governed by the vagaries of 'that

---

13   Smith, op. cit., pp. 494, 518.

insidious and crafty animal otherwise known as a statesman or legislator'; it can be taken hostage by interest groups; and could easily degenerate into tit-for-tat protectionist retaliation. All this can be short-circuited by unilateral trade liberalisation ('Just Do It', in Nike brand terminology), to the benefit of consumers and efficient producers alike. According to Lord Robbins, 'From Adam Smith onwards, the classical tradition in regard to retaliation had been quite definitely that it was seldom worth the candle; and while the matter had not been talked about at great length, the general tone of the literature certainly favoured a unilateral progress to free trade.'[14]

Hume and Smith: international relations

In terms of international relations, Hume and Smith were economic liberals but political realists. They advocated free trade, but took as given a state of international political anarchy, i.e. a system of sovereign nation-states without overarching international government. This stands in contrast to other economic liberals such as Kant, Cobden and later Robbins and Hayek, who looked forward to the day when national governments would be limited and restrained by 'international authorities' and 'world government'.[15]

Hume and Smith, though living in a different time and context, were sober realists who believed that people's patriotic attachment would not extend beyond the nation-state, and that 'global

---

14 Lionel Robbins, *Robert Torrens and the Evolution of Classical Economics*, Macmillan, London, 1958, p. 255.
15 See Lionel Robbins, *Economic Planning and International Order*, Macmillan, London, 1936; F. A. Hayek, *The Road to Serfdom*, Routledge, London, 1944, pp. 163–76.

governance' (as we would now call it) is too artificial and unreal-istic. Hence Adam Smith's reference to the wealth of *nations*, and his advocacy of free markets and free trade in terms of *national* interest. As he saw it, governments unilaterally liberalise trade in the national interest, and others would (or might) follow unilater-ally, in their own interests, when they saw the benefits of such a policy. Both Hume and Smith envisaged international economic integration through markets ('globalisation' in today's terms), but alongside an enduring international political system of nation-states. Governance, rather than going global, would continue to reside primarily at the national level.

Free trade versus protection: nineteenth-century developments[16]

The second half of the nineteenth century was free trade's golden age. In the 1840s Britain switched to unilateral free trade, whose anchor and emblem were the repeal of the Corn Laws. Then followed waves of liberalisation and deregulation that took Britain to almost complete free trade, and kept it there right until World War I. A phalanx of interests – manufacturers, the City of London, the newly enfranchised and unionised working classes – and an impregnable intellectual and political consensus underpinned British free trade in practice.

It was very different outside Britain. Protectionism, not free trade, was the norm on the European continent (except for a

16   This section draws on Irwin, op. cit., chs 6, 7, 8; Robbins, *A History of Economic Thought*, op. cit., lectures 17–25; Schumpeter, op. cit., part III, chs 2–5; Jacob Viner, *Studies in the Theory of International Trade*, George Allen and Unwin, London, 1937. Also see Anthony Howe, *Free Trade and Liberal England, 1846–1946*, Clarendon, Oxford, 1997.

brief interlude in the 1860s and 1870s), in the USA and even in the British self-governing colonies of Canada and Australia. This was reflected in the world of ideas. While mercantilist thought was marginalised in Britain, it endured and held sway in Europe and the USA. Alexander Hamilton and Friedrich List powerfully advocated infant-industry protection to jump-start industrialisation in the USA and Germany. The German Historical School saw protectionism, and mercantilism more generally, in the frame of nation- and state-building – *raison d'état*, in other words.

Such arguments were political and economic in flavour, but, like pre-Adam Smith mercantilism, they were mostly devoid of solid economic analysis. Even within mainstream English classical economics, however, there was, according to Jacob Viner, 'a protectionist skeleton in the free-trade closet'. Robert Torrens developed the terms-of-trade argument in favour of protection, or at least reciprocity, in trade policy. This was later refined into the theory of the 'optimum tariff'. John Stuart Mill and Alfred Marshall conceded the case for temporary protection of infant industries in emerging, industrialising countries.

Nevertheless, while most English classical economists accepted limited *theoretical* departures from the free-trade presumption, they strongly opposed protectionism *in practice*. It was bound to be hijacked by producer interests, and invite tit-for-tat retaliation. To J. S. Mill, protection is 'an organised system of pillage of the many by the few'. And to F. Y. Edgeworth, 'direct use of theory is likely to be small. But it is to be feared that its abuse will be considerable … Let us admire the skill of the analyst, but label the subject of his investigation POISON'.[17]

---

17   Quoted in Irwin, op. cit., p. 114.

Now turn back to the free-trade side of the ledger. English classical economists took the baton from Scottish moral philosophers. From Ricardo onwards, they overhauled and refined economic analysis on trade, payments, prices, wages, production and distribution. On international trade, they paid less attention than Smith and Hume to dynamic and institutional factors, and adopted highly simplified assumptions, moving away from a rough-and-ready but realistic model of the economy to one based on perfect competition.

Despite these shifts in relatively narrow and technical economic analysis, there was continuity in broad political economy: the nineteenth-century English economists and their fellow-travellers generally shared the classical-liberal 'framework assumptions' of their Scottish forebears.

First, they had a cosmopolitan outlook. Free trade, they thought, is conducive to international peace. Many stretched this belief to the point of naivety. Notably, Richard Cobden believed that free trade could substitute for military force and other means of power to preserve the global pax. Hume and Smith were not so credulous.

Second, the English classical economists vigorously defended free trade in the round, on economic *and* political grounds. Their strong preference was for unilateral free trade, not reciprocity. And free trade was coupled strongly with laissez-faire at home, a limited, 'knave-proof' state (i.e. one protected from rent-seeking interests), sacrosanct property rights (including those of foreigners), Gladstonian public finance (low taxation, low expenditure and budget balance), and the gold standard. The package formed a mid-Victorian social contract of sorts. As Schumpeter said, 'free trade [in nineteenth-century Britain] is but an element of a comprehensive system of economic policy and should never be discussed in isolation'.[18] It was a moral and political attitude, an integral part of a wider system of economic liberalism.

Free trade versus protection: twentieth-century developments[19]

Between 1914 and 1945, the nineteenth-century economic system was ripped apart and shredded. It was replaced by rampant protectionism, competing currency blocs, exchange controls and generally spiralling government intervention. The Soviet Union and then Nazi Germany were turned into hermetically sealed centrally planned economies.

Post-1945, the USA led the attempt to establish a new liberal international economic order. This was an exercise in *partial* restoration. The objective was to return to a world of open trade and stable payments, but with sizeable exceptions and 'safety valves'. There was no intention to return to full-blown free trade and a rigid gold standard. That was because 'Smith abroad', i.e. freer trade, had to be reconciled with 'Keynes at home', the label for greater government intervention in the domestic economy. Lastly, new international organisations such as the International Monetary Fund (IMF), the World Bank and the GATT were created to manage this compromise between international openness and domestic intervention.

Mainstream economic thinking on international trade

---

18 Schumpeter, op. cit., p. 398.
19 This section draws on Irwin, op. cit., chs 12–15; Jagdish Bhagwati, *Free Trade Today*, Princeton University Press, Princeton, NJ, 2002; Deepak Lal, *Reviving the Invisible Hand: The Case for Classical Liberalism in the Twenty-first Century*, Princeton University Press, Princeton, NJ, 2006, chs 1–3.

reflected these real-world transformations. The post-1945 theory of commercial policy decoupled free trade from laissez-faire. James Meade, Harry Johnson, Jagdish Bhagwati and others argued that free trade is compatible with a series of targeted 'first-best' interventions to correct domestic market failures. For example, trade protection to promote infant industries is inefficient and costly. Far better to stick to free trade, but use targeted subsidies or other domestic instruments to rectify market failures such as undeveloped financial markets or deficient skill levels in the labour market. But the main point is that free trade was no longer considered part of the bigger classical-liberal package of small government and free markets: it became regarded as compatible with bigger government and the mixed economy.

Arguments for protection were virulent in the first half of the twentieth century, and continued to have force thereafter. After 1945, mercantilist thinking was especially potent in newly decolonised 'underdeveloped' countries. High levels of protection, in the context of escalating government intervention, were justified to promote infant industries, preserve domestic stability, protect national security and secure better positions in the international political pecking order. Soviet central planning, not the Western market economy, was the preferred model. Like mercantilism in previous eras, this was an exercise in nation-state-building. Milder mercantilism prevailed in the West and in the emerging tiger economies of East Asia. There international trade and capital flows were progressively liberalised, but mercantilism found an outlet in policies to promote 'strategic' industries.

The climate of ideas shifted in favour of freer markets alongside the breakdown of the Keynesian consensus in the West, and in reaction to the failure of import substitution and other *dirigiste* policies in the developing world. The collapse of Soviet-type economies delivered the *coup de grâce* to command-and-control economics. Developing countries and countries in transition witnessed widespread and radical liberalisation of trade and capital flows, following what had already been done in the West.

Nevertheless, protectionism, albeit in muted form, remains popular in the West and in the rest of the world. Many protectionist ideas – accumulating trade surpluses, protecting infant industries, securing national positions in what is regarded as zero-sum international competition – hark back to traditional mercantilism. They are products of pre-analytic, pop-internationalist, do-it-yourself economics, bereft of sound economic analysis and of supporting real-world evidence, though that does not make them less popular or politically influential.

That still leaves arguments for protection that have emerged from within mainstream economics. Several have cropped up over the course of the twentieth century. All justify departures from free trade due to the incidence of international or domestic market failures. These have ranged from increasing returns to scale, wage differentials and unemployment to, more recently, strategic interaction among firms in oligopolistic industries. In some cases, protectionism remains the wrong answer, even in theory. For example, it is better to tackle unemployment through labour-market policies than by slapping on a tariff. In other cases, theoretical assumptions can be narrow and unrealistic when applied to real-world conditions. Not least, they demand high levels of information, intelligence and competence from government. This is true of 'strategic trade policy'.

Does government have the knowledge and capability to target strategic sectors and administer the right doses of protection to achieve desired results? Can it be insulated from interest-group capture? Will other governments retaliate, possibly threatening national welfare gains from protection? The free trader's answer would echo Jacob Viner, who concluded that 'these conditions are sufficiently restrictive in combination to guarantee, I am convinced, that the scope for nationally profitable long-run protection is, in practice, very narrowly limited'.[20] John Maynard Keynes summed it up thus: '[Protectionism] is a treacherous instrument for the attainment of its ostensible objective since private interest, administrative incompetence and the intrinsic difficulty of the task may divert it into producing results directly opposed to those intended.'[21]

Conclusion

The theoretical case for free trade is strong and compelling. On the economic front, free trade delivers short-term (static) gains through specialisation according to comparative advantage; and longer-term (dynamic) gains through economies of scale and technology transfer, among other sources. On the political front, it contributes to peaceful international relations. Both economic and political arguments for free trade repose on the foundation of individual freedom – the freedom of people to transact within and across borders. Thus Adam Smith's 'natural liberty' is free trade's bedrock.

Most protectionist arguments are mercantilist old wine in new bottles: they are economic nonsense. But there are more solid theoretical arguments for protection where significant domestic

---

20 Viner, *Studies in the Theory of International Trade*, op. cit., p. 298.
21 Quoted in Irwin, op. cit., p. 199.

or international market failures can be identified. Even these arguments, however, e.g. for an optimum tariff or strategic trade policy, fail the reality test almost all the time. Their assumptions are very restrictive and politically naive. They presume too much government intelligence and capability, and overlook the probability of interest-group capture.

Nevertheless, one cannot help feeling that the modern economic case for free trade, based on neoclassical welfare economics, is too narrow and mechanical, and maybe a little unreal. It is not compelling enough. First, free-trade theory has highly simplified assumptions such as no cross-border factor mobility and zero transport costs. But distance and geography still make a difference to international trade; and international capital mobility (much more than international labour mobility) is an engine of global economic integration. Second, standard theory emphasises the static gains from trade, but says little or nothing about the dynamic gains from trade and their institutional foundations. Third, the post-1945 theory of commercial policy assumes implicitly that governments can intervene intelligently to remedy market failures. Fourth, and in parallel with the post-1945 institutional set-up for the world economy, it also assumes a neat division between what is 'international' (the *dominium* of free trade) and what is 'domestic' (the *imperium* of government intervention). But modern globalisation is thinning and blurring these international–domestic boundaries. Lastly, by decoupling free trade from laissez-faire, the defence of free trade has been cut off from the general case for free markets, limited government and economic freedom.

In light of such reservations, there are strong grounds to return to eighteenth- and nineteenth-century roots, and to put the general case for free trade back in a *classical-liberal* framework. Free trade should be recoupled with laissez-faire: it should be part and parcel of the wider case for free markets, limited government and economic freedom. Its dynamic, institutional features should be emphasised. Rather than maintaining an artificial and increasingly untenable separation between domestic and international spheres, the links between free trade and market-oriented domestic policies should also be emphasised. Finally, free trade should be seen bottom-up, more in terms of unilateral national action and competitive emulation, and less as a top-down product of international organisations and reciprocal bargaining.[22]

These are all elements of a 21st-century vision for free trade. To this I will return in the concluding chapter. But it is now time to shift to real-world trade-policy developments. That is the subject of the next four chapters.

---

22 See Lal, op. cit., especially ch 3. Also see Brink Lindsey, *Against the Dead Hand: The Uncertain Struggle for Global Capitalism*, John Wiley, Washington, DC, 2002.

3 THE POLITICAL ECONOMY OF
   TRADE POLICY

*To expect, indeed, that the freedom of trade should ever be entirely
restored ... is as absurd as to expect that an Oceana or Utopia
should ever be established ... Not only the prejudices of the publick,
but what is much more unconquerable, the private interests of
many individuals, irresistibly oppose it.*

ADAM SMITH, *THE WEALTH OF NATIONS*

*It tells them of freedom, and how freedom was won, and what
freedom has done for them, and it points the way to other paths of
freedom which yet lie open before them.*

JOHN BRIGHT
(ON THE REPEAL OF THE CORN LAWS)

In the last six decades, expanding international trade and capital
flows have progressively reintegrated the world economy in
evermore complex ways. Policy and technological innovation have
combined to produce what we now call economic globalisation.
Post-1945 trade policy has been a constant battle between freer-
trade and protectionist forces. Generally, liberalisation has been
the trend, but it has coexisted uneasily with varieties of protectionism that have always assumed new and potent forms. Free
traders, in the spirit of John Bright's stirring words, were at their
most optimistic in the 1980s and 1990s when liberalisation spread

fast across the developing world and the ex-command economies. Since then a note of caution and pessimism has set in, echoing perhaps the sober Scottish realism of Adam Smith.

This chapter tries to make sense of modern trade-policy developments, especially the acceleration of trade and foreign-investment liberalisation in developing countries since the early 1980s. Its accent is on political economy, drawing on country examples and comparisons to show how politics interacted with economic conditions and shaped the relative success or otherwise of reforms. This exercise is also intended to shed light on the prospects for further external liberalisation in current conditions, at a time when the 'Washington Consensus' attracts greater scepticism than it did in the 1980s and 1990s, and when the momentum of liberalisation has slowed down. How necessary is further liberalisation of trade and foreign direct investment? What obstacles lie in its path? What are its political requisites? What are the links with domestic economic reforms? What is the balance between unilateral liberalisation and reciprocity (liberalisation through trade negotiations and agreements with donors)?

The first section of this chapter sets the scene by looking at the global climate for external liberalisation, including debates revolving around the Washington Consensus. The next section looks at the record of trade and foreign direct investment (FDI) liberalisation across the developing world. This is followed by a framework to analyse the political economy of trade-policy reform. The following section looks at 'multi-track' trade policy conducted, often simultaneously, on unilateral, bilateral, regional and multilateral tracks. The chapter concludes with lessons for future liberalisation in developing countries.

The global climate for external liberalisation

There is less appetite for further liberalisation and associated structural reforms now compared with the heyday of the Washington Consensus in the 1980s and 1990s. Reforms have not been reversed, but their forward momentum has slowed. Governments are more sceptical and defensive about further liberalisation; and there has been relatively little in the way of 'second-generation' reforms (in domestic trade-related regulations and institutions) to underpin external liberalisation and boost competition.

This applies both to the West and to most developing-country regions. In the developed world, pervasive agricultural protectionism continues, with an admixture of new protectionism directed against China. The West has no *grand project* for liberalisation in the early 21st century to compare with the Reagan and Thatcher reforms in the 1980s, or the EU's Single Market programme in the late 1980s and early 1990s. Eastern European countries are suffering from 'reform fatigue' after their accession to the EU. This is also the state of play in much of Latin America, Africa, South Asia and South-East Asia. It is true of leading developing countries, notably Brazil, Mexico, South Africa and India. All have their real bursts of trade-and-FDI liberalisation behind them. In Russia, liberalisation has been put into reverse gear. This has also happened in other resource-rich countries enjoying a revenue windfall, such as Venezuela and Bolivia. Overall, protectionist flare-ups and lack of reform momentum in the West have reinforced the slowdown of liberalisation outside the West.

China is the exception: liberalisation proceeded apace before and after WTO accession, in what has been the biggest opening of an economy the world has ever seen. Domestic political conditions for further liberalisation are, however, now more difficult. Vietnam has followed in China's tracks, with internal and external liberalisation accelerating in the run-up to its WTO accession in 2006.

A variety of factors accounts for scepticism about further liberalisation today. There is much anxiety about globalisation, despite record growth across the world in the last five years. Macroeconomic crises provided windows of opportunity for fast and furious liberalisation in the 1980s and 1990s, but that has not happened since the Asian and other financial crises of the late 1990s. Indeed, the latter may have brought about a popular backlash, and certainly induced more caution regarding further liberalisation. Also, further liberalisation entails tackling border and, increasingly, domestic regulatory barriers in politically sensitive areas such as agriculture and services. Inevitably, this runs up against more powerful interest-group opposition than was the case with previous waves of (mainly industrial-goods) liberalisation. Individuals matter too: the new century has not yet brought forth a Cobden, Gladstone, Erhard, Thatcher or Reagan to champion free markets or free trade.

Not least, the climate of ideas has changed, for prevailing weather conditions have become more inclement since the Washington Consensus reached its zenith only a decade ago. There is, now as before, an extreme anti-globalisation critique, a root-and-branch rejection of capitalism. But this is street theatre on the fringe. Of greater political importance is a more mainstream critique that accepts the reality of the market economy and globalisation, but rejects the comprehensive liberalisation associated (perhaps unfairly) with the Washington Consensus.

Critics point to tenuous links between liberalisation, openness, growth and poverty reduction; wider inequalities within and between countries that result from globalisation; the damaging effects of large and sudden trade liberalisation in developing countries; the renewed emphasis on aid to poorer developing countries, without which trade liberalisation will not work; the need for developed-country liberalisation while retaining developing-country protectionism; and the need for more flexible international rules to allow developing-country governments to pursue selective industrial policies, especially to promote infant industries.[1] Lastly, there is the pervasive fear – in the South as much as in the North – of being run over by an unstoppable Chinese export juggernaut.

It is important to confront the liberalisation sceptics and industrial interventionists head on; to defend liberalisation to date, while accepting that its record is mixed; to make the case for further liberalisation; and to identify the political conditions that might make it succeed. Protectionism and industrial-policy intervention have mostly failed across the developing world: history, not just theory, should be a warning not to go down this route again.

---

1   See Joseph Stiglitz, *Globalisation and Its Discontents*, Allen Lane, London, 2002; Ha-Joon Chang, *Kicking Away the Ladder: Development Strategy in Historical Perspective*, Anthem Press, London, 2002; Isabel Grunberg, Inge Kaul and M. Stern (eds), *Global Public Goods: International Co-operation in the 21st Century*, Oxford University Press, New York and Oxford, 1999; Oxfam, *Rigged Rules and Double Standards: Trade, Globalisation and the Fight against Poverty*, Oxfam International, Oxford, 2002, *www.maketradefair.com*; Dani Rodrik, 'Trading in illusions', *Foreign Policy*, March/April 2001, *www.foreignpolicy.com/issue_marapr_2001/rodrick. html*; Dani Rodrik, *The New Global Economy and Developing Countries: Making Openness Work*, Overseas Development Council, Washington, DC, 1998; Jeffrey Sachs, *The End of Poverty: How We Can Make It Happen in Our Lifetime*, Penguin, London, 2005.

First, in-depth country studies by the Organisation for Economic Cooperation and Development (OECD), the National Bureau of Economic Research (NBER) and the World Bank, going back to the 1970s and 1980s, suggest strongly that countries with more liberal trade policies have more open economies and grow faster than those with more protectionist policies. These are much more reliable than superficial cross-country regression analyses.[2] That said, even most of the latter point to large gains from trade liberalisation.[3]

Putting together calculations done by the World Bank and Angus Maddison, a snapshot of the developing world in the year 2000 reveals the following. There are about twenty-five 'new-globalising' developing countries (the World Bank's term) with a total population of about 3 billion. Since 1980, this group registered massive increases in their trade-to-GDP ratios and real per capita incomes, alongside big cuts in levels of tariff protection. In the same period, over fifty 'less-globalised' developing countries, with a combined population of about 1.5 billion, saw stagnant trade-to-GDP ratios, a modest increase in real per capita incomes, alongside relatively modest cuts in average import tariffs. The – overwhelmingly Asian – new globalisers have also seen dramatic reductions in poverty and improvements in human-welfare

2   Jagdish Bhagwati and T. N. Srinivasan, 'Outward-orientation and development: are revisionists right?', Yale University Economic Growth Center Discussion Paper no. 806, 17 September 1999; Deepak Lal and H. Myint, *The Political Economy of Poverty, Equity and Growth: A Comparative Study*, Clarendon Press, Oxford, 1996.

3   See, for example, Jeffrey Sachs and Andrew Warner, 'Economic reform and the process of global integration', Brookings Papers on Economic Activity, 1, 1995; L. Alan Winters, 'Trade liberalisation and economic performance: an overview', *Economic Journal*, February 2004; L. Alan Winters et al., 'Trade liberalisation and poverty', *Journal of Economic Literature*, March 2004.

indicators (such as adult literacy, infant mortality, life expectancy and nutritional intake).[4]

Second, it is not true that globalisation 'excludes' certain developing countries. Rather globalisation provides an enabling environment that some countries have taken advantage of and others have not. New globalisers in East Asia, South Asia (first Sri Lanka, and now India), central and eastern Europe, Latin America (notably Chile) and elsewhere have reaped the benefits through more market-oriented policies and institutions. They are narrowing the wealth gap with the West. This is why global poverty has been massively reduced (especially as a percentage of world population, and even in absolute numbers, despite a growing world population). Political disorder, macroeconomic instability, insecure property rights, rampant government intervention and high external protection have kept other countries 'non-globalised' and have thereby retarded growth and development. Most of these countries are cursed with dysfunctional or failed states run by venal, thuggish, even murderous elites. None of this is 'caused' by globalisation.[5]

Third, non-governmental organisations (NGOs) and developing-country governments have been clamouring for one-sided liberalisation in the Doha Round. Their interpretation of 'development' in the Doha Development Agenda is that it behoves developed countries to liberalise in areas that are protected against

4 World Bank, *Globalisation, Growth and Poverty: Building an Inclusive World Economy*, World Bank, Washington, DC, 2002, p. 34, especially Table 1.1; Angus Maddison, *The World Economy: Historical Statistics*, OECD, Paris, 2003.

5 Martin Wolf, *Why Globalisation Works: The Case for the Global Market Economy*, Yale University Press, New Haven, CT, 2004, ch. 9; David Henderson, 'Globalisation, economic progress and New Millennium Collectivism', *World Economics*, 5(3), July/September 2004, pp. 52–8.

labour-intensive developing-country exports. But developing countries should not reciprocate with their own liberalisation. What Oxfam and others fail to say is that developing countries' own protectionist policies harm them even more than developed-country barriers. The World Bank estimates that 80 per cent of the developing-country gain from worldwide agricultural liberalisation would come from developing countries' liberalisation of their highly protected agricultural markets. It is unskilled rural labour – the poorest of the poor – who would gain most as such liberalisation would reduce the anti-agricultural bias in domestic economies.[6]

Fourth, the historical record is not kind to 'hard' industrial policies of the infant-industry variety. Infant-industry success in nineteenth-century USA and Germany is contested. In East Asia, its record is mixed at best in Japan, South Korea and Taiwan; non-existent in free-trade Hong Kong and Singapore; and failed in South-East Asia (e.g. national car policies in Malaysia and Indonesia). In north-east Asia, there is scant evidence to show that protection of infants actually led to higher social rates of return and higher overall productivity growth.[7] South-East Asia's conspicuous success is in FDI-led electronics exports – a result of drastically lower tariffs and an open door to inward investment. China, like South-East Asia, has grown fast through FDI-led exports, not infant-industry protection. Arguably, other factors – political and macroeconomic stability, competitive exchange rates, private property rights, openness to the world economy, education and

6   Oxfam, op. cit.; M. D. Ingco and J. D. Nash (eds), *Agriculture and the WTO: Creating a Trading System for Development*, World Bank, Washington, DC, 2004.

7   World Bank, *The East Asian Miracle*, World Bank, Washington, DC, 1993; I. M. D. Little, 'Trade and industrialisation revisited', in I. M. D. Little, *Collection and Recollections*, Clarendon, Oxford, 1999.

infrastructure – were much more important to East Asian success than 'picking winners'. Finally, infant-industry protection in Latin America, South Asia and Africa has been a disaster not dissimilar to industrial planning in ex-command economies. Protected infants sooner or later ran into severe problems; and governments continued to subsidise and protect perpetual children. Such incestuous government–business links provided a fertile breeding ground for corruption. Besides, most developing-country markets are too small to support infant-industry promotion; and their states are too weak, incompetent and corrupt to efficiently administer the complex instruments required.

Protectionism in the world: unfinished business

Protectionism remains high around the world, even after six decades of liberalisation, first in developed countries and then in developing countries. There are still pockets of developed-country protection. These include agricultural subsidies, peak tariffs and tariff escalation in agriculture and manufactures, together with anti-dumping duties, assorted regulatory barriers such as onerous product standards, and high restrictions on the cross-border movement of workers. These pockets of protection continue to damage developing-country growth prospects.

But developing countries' own protection on almost all these counts is much higher and more damaging. Average applied tariffs in developing countries are more than double those in developed countries, with much higher bound rates in the WTO (Table 1). South Asia, sub-Saharan Africa, the Middle East and North Africa have higher average tariffs than East Asia, Latin America and eastern Europe (Table 2). Bound and applied tariffs in agriculture are significantly higher than they are in manufactures. Developing countries have become bigger users of anti-dumping actions than developed countries (Figure 1). A few developing countries – notably India – have become much more frequent users of anti-dumping actions (Figure 2). Developing countries, with the exception of countries in transition and those that have recently acceded to the WTO, have far fewer multilateral commitments in services than developed countries (Figure 3). There has been a general increase in the use of technical, food-safety and other standards that affect trade, as indicated by the number of measures notified under the WTO's Technical Barriers to Trade (TBT) and Sanitary and Phytosanitary Standards (SPS) agreements. This is one – admittedly very rough – indication of regulatory barriers to trade. Developed countries account for over half of TBT and SPS measures notified, but what is also striking is the increasing number of measures notified by developing countries (Figures 4 and 5).

Thus there is much unfinished business in terms of liberalising trade, capital flows and the cross-border movement of labour in the developing world. That said, external liberalisation is no panacea. In the short run, trade liberalisation reduces the anti-import, anti-export bias of trade taxes. That is the prelude to dynamic gains – including those from trade-related inward investment – that result in productivity improvements and growth. Capturing these gains, however, depends on additional factors: initial conditions for reform, including a country's factor endowments and historical legacy; complementary domestic market-based reforms; and the state of and improvement in domestic institutions. The connection between opening to the world economy and domestic economic and institutional reform is particularly important: it is this which explains much of the variation in economic performance in the developing world. As I argued in the last chapter, this is not a new insight: David Hume and Adam Smith strongly linked free trade (broadly defined to include cross-border flows of capital and people) to domestic institutions and growth, all on the canvas of the long-run progress of commercial society. But this also begs difficult political questions. In essence, successful external opening depends crucially on domestic politics and institutional capacity. Here there are very large and arguably increasing differences within the developing world.

Table 1 **Bound and applied tariff rates**

	Bound		Applied	
	Developed economies	Developing economies	Developed economies	Developing economies
All goods	17.8	43.6	5.5	11.8
Agriculture	24.3	60.6	9.5	16.3
Manufactures	16.7	32.5	4.8	11.0

Note: Developed and developing economies by World Bank definitions. Developed economies: category 3–4 (2002–04) and developing economies: category 1–2 (1998–2004).
Source: World Bank Trade Databases: http://siteresources.worldbank.org/INTRES/Resources/469232–1107449512766/tar2005a.xls

Trade-policy reforms: the recent experience, with country examples

Trade liberalisation has several definitions. Trade economists speak of moving to 'neutrality' of government intervention as between tradable and non-tradable sectors of the economy. They also speak of 'getting prices right' by aligning domestic prices with world prices of tradable goods. More broadly conceived, free

Table 2 **Tariff rates in different regions**

Country group or region	Applied	Bound	Agriculture (Applied)	Manufactures (Applied)
High-income economies	5.5	17.8	10.6	3.3
Latin America and the Caribbean	9.9	41.2	14.9	9.0
East Asia and Pacific	10.5	29.5	16.8	10.5
South Asia	17.8	66.5	19.1	17.2
Europe and Central Asia	7.8	13.2	14.0	6.7
Middle East and North Africa	18.0	34.6	22.5	16.9
Sub-Saharan Africa	13.4	61.5	17.2	12.9

Note: The numbers are unweighted averages in per cent from 1998 to 2004.
Regional definitions by the World Bank: http://web.worldbank.org/WBSITE/
EXTERNAL/DATASTATISTICS/0,,contentMDK:20421402~pagePK:64133150~piPK:64
133175~theSitePK:239419,00.html.
Source: World Bank trade databases: http://siteresources.worldbank.org/INTRES/
Resources/469232–1107449512766/tar2005a.xls

(or free-ish) trade means the freedom to engage in international transactions, without discrimination.[8] This exists nowhere – not even in Hong Kong, which maintains tight restrictions on immigration, though it is fully open to trade in goods and capital flows, and largely open to trade in services. If non-discrimination is the relevant criterion, all countries are still far from free trade, indeed more so than was the case in the late nineteenth century.

Nevertheless, there has been a distinct liberalisation trend in developing countries in recent decades.[9] Cross-border trade and

8   David Henderson, 'International economic integration: progress, prospects and implications', *International Affairs*, 64(4), 1992, p. 635.
9   On the record of trade and FDI liberalisation as part of larger packages of market-based reforms in developing countries and countries in transition, see John Williamson (ed.), *The Political Economy of Policy Reform*, Institute for Inter-

Figure 1   **Anti-dumping measures**

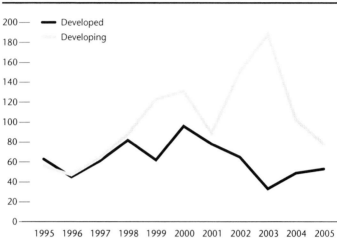

Note: Anti-dumping measures: by reporting Member. Classification of countries by World Bank definitions
Source: WTO, http://www.wto.org/english/tratop_e/adp_e/adp_stattab7_e.xls

national Economics, Washington, DC, 1993; Pedro Pablo Kuczynski and John Williamson (eds), *After the Washington Consensus: Restarting Growth and Reform in Latin America*, Institute for International Economics, Washington, DC, 2004; Lal and Myint, op. cit.; Judith Dean, 'The trade-policy revolution in developing countries', *The World Economy, Global Trade Policy 1995*; Zdenek Drabek and Sam Laird, 'The New Liberalism: trade-policy developments in emerging markets', *Journal of World Trade*, 32(5), 1998, pp. 241–69; David Henderson, *The Changing Fortunes of Economic Liberalism: Yesterday, Today and Tomorrow*, Institute of Economic Affairs, London, 1998; Constantine Michalopoulos, *Developing Countries and the WTO*, Palgrave, London, 2001. On trade-policy trends in Asia, see Razeen Sally, 'Trade policy in Asia', ECIPE Policy Brief, 1, 2007, *www.ecipe.org/pdf/Policy-brief_0107.pdf*; Razeen Sally, 'Chinese trade policies in wider Asian perspective', in *Globalisation and Economic Growth in China*, ed. Yang Yao and Linda Yueh, World Scientific Publishing, London, 2006, pp. 181–233; Razeen Sally and Rahul Sen, 'Whither trade policies in southeast Asia? The wider Asian and global context', *ASEAN Economic Bulletin*, 22(1), April 2005, pp. 92–115, Special Issue: 'Revisiting trade policies in southeast Asia', ed. Razeen Sally and Rahul Sen.

Figure 2   **Most frequent users of anti-dumping measures**

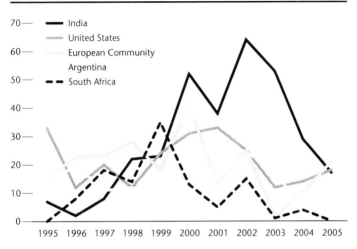

Note: Anti-dumping measures: by reporting member
Source: WTO, http://www.wto.org/english/tratop_e/adp_e/adp_stattab7_e.xls

capital flows – though not of people – have become freer. There is less discrimination between domestic and international transactions. Domestic prices of tradable goods and services are closer to world prices (though this is less the case in services than in goods). Import and export quotas, licensing requirements, state trading monopolies and other non-tariff barriers have been drastically reduced. Tariffs have been simplified and reduced. So have foreign-exchange controls, with unified exchange rates and much greater currency convertibility, especially on current-account transactions. Foreign direct investment has been liberalised, with fewer restrictions on entry, ownership, establishment and operation in the domestic economy. And services sectors have been

Figure 3   **Distribution of GATS commitments across groups of members**

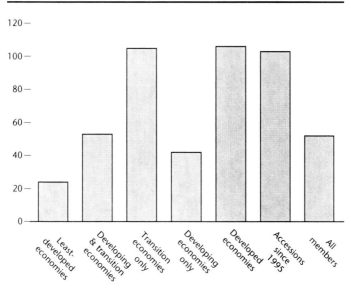

Source: WTO (Staff Working Paper ERSD-2005-01) http://www.wto.org/english/res_e/reser_e/
ersd200501_e.doc

opened to international competition through FDI liberalisation, privatisation and domestic deregulation. Overall, trade and FDI in manufactured goods has been liberalised most; trade and FDI in services were liberalised later, and to a much lesser extent; and trade liberalisation in agriculture has lagged behind. Lastly, trade and FDI liberalisation has taken place in the context of wide-ranging macro and microeconomic market-based reforms – roughly the 'stabilisation and liberalisation' package of the Washington Consensus, as described by John Williamson.

Cumulatively, this has been a veritable policy revolution

Figure 4   **Number of notified SPS measures**
1995–2001

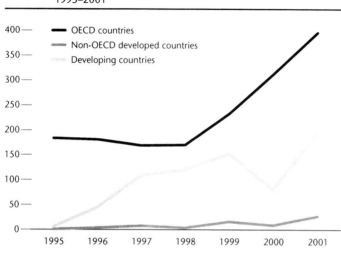

Source: OECD (2002) Joint Working Paper Party on Agriculture and Trade, COM/TD/AGR/
WP(2002)21/FINAL

in developing countries and countries in transition. Before the 1980s, the 80 per cent of the world's population who live outside the West lived overwhelmingly in countries with high levels of external protection, in addition to pervasive government intervention at home. By the mid-1990s, most of these people lived in much more open economies, in terms of both domestic and international commerce. Average applied tariffs in developing countries declined from 30 per cent in 1985 to 11 per cent in 2005 (Figure 6). Core non-tariff barriers declined correspondingly in all developing-country regions (Table 3). The bulk of regulatory changes on inward investment has been more favourable to

Figure 5   **Number of notified TBT measures, 1995–2001**

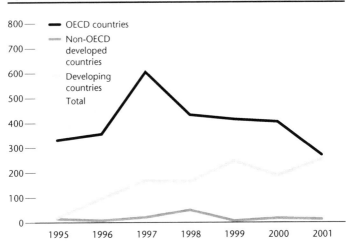

Source: OECD (2003) Joint Working Paper Party on Agriculture and Trade, COM/TD/AGR/
WP(2002)70/FINAL

FDI (Table 4 shows the number of unfavourable and favourable changes). There has even been a trend in favour of capital-account liberalisation: 70 per cent of the developing countries in the IMF maintain capital-account restrictions today compared with 85 per cent in the early 1990s (Figure 7).

This liberalisation trend started in Japan in the 1950s, and then spread to South Korea and Taiwan, at a time when most developing countries were tightening regimes of import substitution and other forms of state intervention. The north-east Asian tigers promoted exports through selective liberalisation, while retaining considerable import protection and restrictions on inward investment. Later they gradually liberalised imports and FDI. Hong Kong returned to

Table 3 **Frequency of NTBs in developing countries 1989–2000 (%)**

Region	1989–94	1995–98	2000
East Asia and the Pacific	30.1	16.3	5.5
Latin America and the Caribbean	18.3	8.0	15.3
Middle East and North Africa	43.8	16.6	8.5
South Asia	57.0	58.3	13.3
Sub-Saharan Africa	26.0	10.4	2.3

Note: Figures are regional averages of percentage of tariff lines subject to core NTBs, including all types of quantity restrictions and price administration or control as well as monopolistic trading channels
Source: For 1989–94 and 1995–98: IMF, www.imf.org/external/np/pp/eng/2005/021505.pdf, citing B. Hoekman, 'Economic development and the WTO after Doha', World Bank Policy Research Working Paper no. 2851, Washington, DC, June 2002; for 2000: Cordell Institute, www.cordellhullinstitute.org/TPA/Volume%207%20(2005)/Vol%207,%20No.%202%20-%20Thomas%20Dalsgaard%20on%20Trade%20Reform%20&%20Revenue%20Loss.pdf, citing *Global Monitoring Report 2004*, World Bank, Washington, DC, Table 4.6.

tariff-free trade and a fully open door to investment after the war. Singapore followed, though after a brief flirtation with protection (when part of the Malaysian federation). The other South-East Asian tigers (Malaysia, Thailand, Indonesia and the Philippines) liberalised significantly, on both trade and FDI, from the 1970s. The countries of Indochina started gradual and halting market-based reforms in the 1980s. Vietnam accelerated trade and investment liberalisation in the run-up to its WTO accession in late 2006.

China's historic opening dates back to 1978, but major trade and investment liberalisation took off from the early 1990s. Since then, China has swung from extreme protection to rather liberal trade policies – indeed, very liberal by developing-country standards. The crowning point of China's reforms was its WTO accession in 2001. Its WTO commitments are by far the strongest of any developing country in the WTO.

Table 4 **National regulatory changes on FDI, 1992–2005, by region**

		1992	1993	1994	1995
World	More favourable	77	99	108	106
	Less favourable	–	1	2	6
Developed	More favourable	11	24	17	22
countries	Less favourable	–	–	1	2
Developing	More favourable	49	63	79	62
economies	Less favourable	–	1	1	3
Africa	More favourable	9	12	22	12
	Less favourable	–	–	–	–
Latin America and	More favourable	9	17	14	18
the Caribbean	Less favourable	–			2
West Asia	More favourable	3	8	4	4
	Less favourable	–	–	–	–
South, East and	More favourable	27	26	39	28
South-East Asia	Less favourable	–	1	1	1
Oceania	More favourable	1	–	–	–

Source: UNCTAD

In South Asia, Sri Lanka pioneered external liberalisation in the late 1970s. India's retreat from the 'licence raj' – its equivalent of Soviet-style central planning – began half-heartedly in the 1980s; its decisive opening to the world economy dates back to 1991. Pakistan followed in the late 1990s.

In Latin America, Chile pioneered radical external liberalisation in the 1970s. Other Latin American countries followed in the 1980s (notably Mexico) and 1990s (notably Brazil, Argentina and Peru). African liberalisation was slow in the 1980s and faster in the 1990s. South Africa had a big opening of the economy in the run-up to and after the end of apartheid. The countries of central and eastern Europe and the Baltic states had a 'big bang' transition from central planning to the market after 1989, which

1996	1997	1998	1999	2000	2001	2002	2003	2004	2005
98	134	136	130	147	193	234	218	234	164
16	16	9	9	3	14	12	24	36	41
25	36	20	27	29	38	54	45	54	40
3	6	4	5	-	3	2	3	6	4
58	87	109	78	105	127	144	139	144	92
10	5	3	2	2	10	9	20	27	30
15	14	23	16	13	25	21	43	46	42
2	–	1	–	–	3	6	2	11	11
14	30	13	17	29	18	15	16	26	7
1	4	2	2	–	3	2	11	9	14
4	5	18	7	24	26	34	35	34	15
–	–	–	–	1	2	1	4	1	1
25	33	52	37	38	58	74	44	37	28
7	1	–	–	1	2	–	3	6	4
–	5	3	1	1	–		1	1	–

included massive liberalisation of trade and capital flows. This was less the case, and certainly more erratic, in Russia, other parts of the ex-Soviet Union and south-eastern Europe. Liberalisation has, however, recently accelerated in some of these countries, such as Romania, Bulgaria, Georgia and parts of the former Yugoslavia.

Finally, trade and investment liberalisation in the old OECD countries has taken place in small steps since the 1980s – not surprising, since these are largely open economies in which the bulk of liberalisation was done in the 1950s and 1960s. The exceptions are Australia and New Zealand. After over a century of protection, both opened decisively to the world economy in the 1980s.

Figure 6   **Average applied tariff rates in developing countries 1981–2005**, unweighted in %

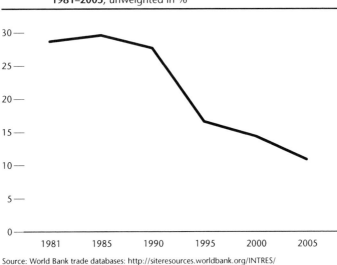

Source: World Bank trade databases: http://siteresources.worldbank.org/INTRES/
Resources/tar2005.xls

Political economy and trade-policy reforms

The politics of economic-policy reform is as much about distribution as it is about wealth generation. This is true of international
politics; it is even truer of domestic politics. Shifts in trade policy
– from protection to openness or vice versa – trigger redistribution of gains and losses between regions (especially between rural
and urban areas), sectors of the economy (agriculture, industry,
services), classes (owners of capital, educated and skilled workers,
semi- and unskilled workers), and even between ethnic groups.
Such disruption, especially in the short term, can be particularly unsettling in developing countries with political instability,
corrupt elites, wide disparities in wealth and influence, meagre

Figure 7   **Countries with capital controls**
% of total IMF membership*

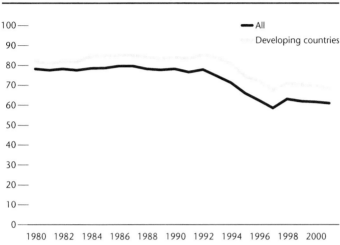

*Based on a simple 1-0 classification (covering all capital account transactions), as provided by the
AREAER. There was a definitional change from 1997 to 1998.
Source: IMF Evolution report The IMF's Approach to Capital Account Liberalization (2005):
http://www.imf.org/external/np/ieo/2005/cal/eng/report.pdf

safety nets, ethnic divides and generally brittle institutions. Hence
trade and other forms of liberalisation take place in a snakepit of
messy and sometimes poisonous politics.

What are the determinants of trade-policy reform, especially in
the direction of liberalisation? What follows is a simple taxonomy
of relevant factors: a) circumstances, especially crises; b) interests;
c) ideas; d) institutions; e) factor endowments.

TRADE POLICY, NEW CENTURY

a) Circumstances/crises

Events, dear boy, events.

HAROLD MACMILLAN

When a man knows he is going to be hanged in a fortnight, it concentrates the mind wonderfully.

DR JOHNSON

The practical politician, official or businessman knows that choices are dictated by responses to often unanticipated events. In reality, major episodes of economic-policy reform have mostly taken place in response to political and/or economic crises. A macroeconomic crisis, with symptoms such as extreme internal or external indebtedness, hyperinflation, a terms-of-trade shock or a severe payments imbalance leading to a plummeting currency, provides the classic backdrop. This is when 'normal politics' is suspended, and when a period of 'extraordinary politics' can provide a window of opportunity for thoroughgoing reforms that would not be possible in 'normal' political circumstances.[10] Examples are legion: Chile in 1973/74; Mexico in 1986; Brazil and Argentina in the early 1990s; South Africa in the mid-1990s; Sri Lanka in 1977; India in 1991; eastern Europe and the former Soviet Union in the early 1990s; Australia and New Zealand in 1983/84.

But the crisis explanation cannot be taken too far. First, a crisis can precipitate swings both ways: sometimes towards liberalisation; sometimes the other way, as happened during

---

10 Stephan Haggard and John Williamson, 'The political conditions for economic reform', in Williamson (ed.), *The Political Economy of Policy Reform*, op. cit., pp. 527–96; Leczek Balcerowicz, *Socialism, Capitalism, Transformation*, Central European University Press, Budapest, 1995.

the Depression in the 1930s, and, to a lesser extent, in the 1970s after the first oil-price shock. Second, different governments act in different ways in response to similar external shocks. Third, a crisis might trigger some reforms, but it is no guarantee of the sustainability of those reforms, nor of further reforms down the line. That is one key difference between the central and eastern European states and the Baltic states, on the one hand, and Russia and other parts of the former Soviet Union, on the other. Lastly, there are counter-examples of gradual, but cumulatively substantial, reforms without a sudden crisis as a triggering mechanism. That is, roughly, the East Asian record.

Why have some countries sustained reforms while others have not? Why have some gone farther than others? What happens to a reform programme post-crisis, when 'normal' political and economic conditions return? These questions demand supplementary explanations.

b) Interests

A good cause seldom triumphs without someone's interest behind it.

JOHN STUART MILL

Mainstream economists, following Adam Smith, tend to rely on an interest-group explanation of trade politics. Free trade is the optimal policy in most circumstances (they say), but protection is more often the result, because organised rent-seeking interests demand protection, and politicians and officials supply it. The benefits of free trade are diffused over the broad majority of consumers, but its costs bear down disproportionately on minority producer interests. The latter, not the former, have the incentive to organise for collective action.[11] In reality, 'iron quadrangles' of politicians, bureaucrats, employers and unions imposed a strait-jacket of protection in developing countries from the 1930s to the 1970s. Mostly this benefited capital-intensive, unionised, urban manufacturing industries producing for the domestic market, at the expense of agriculture and tradable sectors. India's license raj was its most notorious incarnation. In many countries, a crisis was used to overcome interest-group opposition and push through liberalising reforms (as happened in India in 1991).

But what role do interest groups play after an initial burst of external liberalisation, and in post-crisis conditions when 'normal' politics returns? Here the picture differs across countries and regions. In some parts of the world, protectionist coalitions have halted or slowed down liberalisation. This is the case with 'nomenklatura' coalitions in Russia, Ukraine and other parts of the former Soviet Union. Elsewhere, radical opening has triggered major economic shifts in favour of sectors exposed to the world economy. Traditional protectionist interests have been weakened, and countervailing coalitions have emerged. The latter comprise exporters, users of imported inputs, multinationals with global production networks, and cities and regions seeking to be magnets for trade and FDI. These interests lobby for the maintenance and extension of open trade and FDI regimes.[12] This has happened

11   Mancur Olson, *The Logic of Collective Action: Public Goods and the Theory of Groups*, Harvard University Press, Cambridge, MA, 1971; Anne O. Krueger, 'The political economy of the rent-seeking society', *American Economic Review*, 64, 1974, pp. 291–303.

12   Ricardo–Viner and Heckscher–Ohlin models of comparative advantage are used to explain interest-group activity for and against free trade in different countries with different factor endowments. See Jeffrey Frieden and Ronald Rogowski, 'The impact of the international economy on national policies', in Robert Keohane and Helen Milner (eds), *Internationalisation and Domestic Politics*, Cambridge

in strong-liberalising countries in East Asia, eastern Europe and Latin America. It happened in Australia and New Zealand from the early 1980s. It is also evident in India after the 1991 reforms.

c) Ideas

It is the word in season that does much to decide the result.

JOHN STUART MILL

Madmen who hear voices in the air are distilling their frenzy from the academic scribblings of some defunct economist or political philosopher. Indeed the world is ruled by little else.

JOHN MAYNARD KEYNES

It is always difficult to gauge the influence of ideas (or ideology) in policy.[13] But practical observation teaches us that the prevailing climate of ideas, interacting with interests and events, can entrench or sway this or that set of policies. A policy consensus on import substitution, state planning and foreign aid was strongly embedded in developing-country governments and international organisations up to the 1970s. This was buttressed by a post-colonial political ideology of mercantilist state-building, and an interventionist consensus in development economics.[14] This set of ideas was overturned by what came to be called the *Washington*

University Press, Cambridge, 1996; Ronald Rogowski, *Commerce and Coalitions: How Trade Affects Domestic Political Alignments*, Princeton University Press, Princeton, NJ, 1990.

13 On 'ideational' approaches, see Judith Goldstein, *Ideas, Interests and American Trade Policy*, Cornell University Press, Ithaca, NY, 1994.

14 P. T. Bauer, *From Subsistence to Exchange and Other Essays*, Princeton University Press, Princeton, NJ, 2000; Lal and Myint, op. cit.

Consensus, which reflected sea-changes in political ideology and in development economics. The latter returned to classical and neoclassical foundations, emphasising market-based pricing, 'outward orientation', the prevalence of 'government failure' over 'market failure', not to mention a dose of aid scepticism.

Washington Consensus ideas took stronger hold in countries where reforms were substantial, especially in ministries of finance, central banks and presidential/prime-ministerial offices. These agencies tend to be the cockpits of policy reform. But now the climate of ideas has changed somewhat. This does not presage a return to full-blown pre-Washington Consensus thinking. The pendulum, however, is swinging towards more attention to market failure and government intervention, for example to ease back on further liberalisation, expand 'policy space' and promote infant industries, defend 'food security' and increase foreign aid. The question is what effect this is having, and is likely to have, on trade policies.

d) Institutions

In the broad sense, institutions are the steel frame of the economy, its 'formal rules and informal constraints', according to Douglass North. The legal framework governing property rights and contracts, production and consumption comes to mind. 'Formal rules' comprise bankruptcy laws, competition laws, regulations governing financial markets and corporate governance, and much else besides. 'Informal constraints' are (often non-legal) traditions and norms influencing the intersecting worlds of business, government and the law.

Evidently, 'institutions' are much broader and more difficult to pin down than 'policies'; and the two are of course intimately connected. Historically conditioned institutions, domestic and external, set the scene for government action, interest-group lobbying and the influence of ideas. They are the arena for policy choices and their implementation. Making generalisations about institutional constraints on policy choice, and how this might explain differences in national and regional economic performance over time, is notoriously difficult. To what extent must 'good' institutions be in place before 'good' policies can take hold and work their magic? Conversely, to what extent are institutions the result, rather than the cause, of policy choices? These are chicken-and-egg questions.

In the narrow sense, institutions are the organisational map of decision-making at the junction where politics and public policy meet business and society. On trade policy, this map is much more complicated than it used to be. Trade policy is no longer just about a clutch of border instruments, and the preserve of trade ministries. It is increasingly 'trade related', a matter of non-border regulation reaching deep into the domestic economy and its institutions. That is reflected in more complex multilateral, regional and bilateral trade agreements. This brings in agencies across the range of government, and many actors outside government as well. Now the management of trade policy involves: the division of labour between the executive, legislature and judiciary; the lead ministry; other ministries and regulatory agencies with responsibility for trade and trade-related policies; the WTO mission in Geneva; inter-agency coordination within government; the involvement of non-governmental actors, such as business and unions, and now including NGOs and think tanks; and donors and international organisations.

Inasmuch as one can make generalisations about institutions

and trade policy in developing countries, here are a couple. First, it is the more advanced developing countries (in terms of per capita income and human-welfare indicators) which have liberalised more and plugged themselves better into globalisation than other developing countries. They have lower trade and FDI barriers, higher ratios of trade and FDI to GDP, and better-performing tradable sectors of the economy. They also have stronger institutions in the broad sense: better enforcement of property rights and contracts (i.e. the rule of law), better-functioning judiciaries and public administration, better-regulated financial markets, a stronger competition culture, less corruption and so on. This is the divide that separates Chile and a few other Latin American countries, eastern Europe, the north-east Asian and South-East Asian tigers, and a tiny handful of African countries (Mauritius, Botswana and South Africa), from the rest. There are, however, two gigantic anomalies: China and India. Both are still low-income countries with weak institutions (going by some of the indicators mentioned above). Institutional improvements have taken place, but these have lagged well behind big policy shifts – not least lower trade and FDI restrictions – and fast-paced global integration.[15]

Second, looking at institutions in the narrower organisational sense, strong and sustained trade-policy and wider economic-policy reforms were driven, more often than not, by powerful presidential or prime-ministerial offices, ministries of finance and central banks, insulated from blocking pressures in other parts of government and outside government. This was more pronounced

---

15   See the World Bank's governance and business-climate indicators. They point to large institutional and policy differences among developing countries. They also point to relatively weak institutions, as well as the high 'red tape' costs of doing business, in China and India. World Bank, *Doing Business in 2007*, World Bank, Washington, DC, 2006; World Bank governance indicators, *www.worldbank.org*.

in advanced developing countries than elsewhere. These countries also have stronger capacity, in terms of qualified, experienced manpower and other resources, for formulating and implementing trade policy, whether done unilaterally or through international negotiations and agreements. Again, China and India are exceptional: they are low-income countries with relatively weak institutions (in the broad sense), but with relatively strong trade-policy capacity.

e) Factor endowments

Explaining the trajectory of policy reforms is not complete without factoring in the relative mix of land (or natural resources), labour and capital in an economy.[16] We know from recent economic history that the star developing-country performers are from East Asia. These countries had different starting positions; but, at a certain stage of development, relative labour abundance allowed them to break into labour-intensive manufactured exports, which became an engine of growth and in turn aided poverty reduction and human-welfare improvement. Of course, this was not inevitable: it depended on the right policies and improving institutions. South Asia, with similar factor endowments, remained stuck on a low-growth, high-poverty path because it did not adopt market-based policies. Latin American and African countries, on the other hand, are largely land- or resource-abundant and labour-scarce. In the absence of import-substitution policies, they are better able to exploit comparative advantage in land and resources – as Brazil,

---

16 Lal and Myint, op. cit., provide perhaps the best analysis of how factor endowments have influenced the political economy of post-colonial policy reforms in developing countries.

Argentina, Chile, Australia and New Zealand have done in agriculture since they liberalised, and as all the latter and many other countries besides are doing in the present China-driven commodities boom. Thus a simple story based on early 21st-century comparative advantage would point to all-round gains from trade: for technologically advanced and capital-abundant countries in the West; the labour-abundant countries of East and South Asia; and land and resource-abundant countries elsewhere.

But the political economy of factor endowments reveals a different and more problematic story. Arguably, land- and resource-abundant countries are at a structural disadvantage compared with labour-abundant countries. By plugging into global markets for manufacturing, and now labour-intensive services too, the latter seem to be on sustainable growth paths. Labour-intensive exports attract FDI (and the technology and skills that come with it), feed quickly into poverty-reducing, welfare-improving employment, and, more gradually, into better infrastructure and institutions. This creates and strengthens a constellation of interests to support open trade and FDI policies.

On the other hand, land- and resource-abundant countries, given their relatively high price of labour, seem to be crowded out of global manufacturing markets by East Asian (especially Chinese) competition.[17] This leaves them dependent on cyclical and volatile commodities markets. FDI in resource-abundant countries tends to be capital-intensive and generates big rents in not-so-competitive market segments. Often the result is an FDI enclave, without an employment, technology or wealth spillover to the rest of the economy, but with big profits to distribute

17   Wolf, op. cit., pp. 146–9.

among a corrupt local business and political elite. Most countries dependent on resources have the interest-group constellation to squander rents from resource booms, but not to spread wealth and improve governance and institutions. A retreat to protectionism, however, would repeat past mistakes and make matters worse. This is the dilemma inherent in the present 'China-in-Africa' phenomenon. But there are notable exceptions to the 'resource-curse' rule: Chile has successfully exploited comparative advantage in agriculture and resources (mainly copper) through liberal trade policies, while diversifying the economic base and improving institutions. That is also true of Australia and New Zealand.

f) Preliminary summary

In most strong-liberalising countries, a political or macroeconomic crisis has led to a big opening of the economy; new open-economy interest-group constellations have emerged to counter traditional protectionist interests; open-market ideas have become entrenched; and stronger institutions are better able to support and manage open-market policies. Some countries, such as China and others in East Asia, have gone down this path without the catalyst of a macroeconomic crisis. Generally, advanced developing countries have more liberal trade policies, stronger institutions and are more globally integrated than the rest. China and India are the two big exceptions: they have liberalised extensively and integrated fast into the global economy, but with still-weak institutions. Labour-abundant countries in East Asia, and now in South Asia, best fit the big picture of external liberalisation and global integration. The picture looks different in countries that have liberalised less and globalised less. Resource-abundant countries in Latin America, Africa, the Middle East, Russia and other parts of the former Soviet Union are now doing well in the China-driven commodities boom. But their political economy is problematic: their predatory governments and interest groups are geared more to squandering rents than to creating and spreading wealth sustainably.

Multi-track trade policy

Another way of cutting into trade-policy reform is to look at it on several tracks. Some reforms are carried out *unilaterally*; others *reciprocally* through (bilateral, regional or multilateral) trade negotiations, or in agreements with donors. Most developing countries now do trade policy on all these tracks concurrently, though the relative balance differs from country to country.

What follows is a brief summary of the main features of 'multi-track' trade policy in developing countries. Chapters 4, 5 and 6 will flesh out the detail on the WTO, PTAs and unilateral liberalisation, especially in Asia. Foreign aid has also been an important factor in trade-policy reforms – in some countries more than in others. That is also examined in this section.

a) Unilateral liberalisation

This is the Nike strategy ('Just Do It!'). Governments 'liberalise first and negotiate later', as Mart Laar, the former prime minister of Estonia, puts it. In theory, this makes good economic sense. The gain from liberalisation comes from imports, which release domestic resources for more productive uses, including exports, and help to open the door to inward investment.[18] Why, therefore, delay the gain by waiting for cumbersome, bureaucratic trade negotiations to deliver the goods? Unilateral liberalisation can make political sense too, as it can be tailored to local conditions rather than being dictated by 'one-size-fits-all' donor conditionality and international trade agreements.

The British led the way with unilateral free trade in the nineteenth century. The first half of the twentieth century witnessed unilateral protectionism by country after country. Since 1945, most developed countries have liberalised reciprocally, through the GATT and bilateral/regional trade agreements. But most developing-country trade and FDI liberalisation has been done unilaterally, not through trade negotiations. The World Bank estimates that two-thirds of developing-country tariff liberalisation since the early 1980s has been done unilaterally.[19] The strongest liberalisers have been unilateral liberalisers: the East Asian countries, now led by China; Chile and Mexico; the eastern European countries; Australia and New Zealand; and South Africa. Nearly all of India's post-1991 liberalisation has been done unilaterally.

18 There is the theoretical possibility of (usually large) countries being able to exercise long-run market power in international demand for certain goods. This enables them to shift the terms of trade in their favour by means of an 'optimal tariff'. The corollary is that these countries should lower tariffs only if others reciprocate, in order to avoid worsening terms of trade. In reality, very few countries have such long-run market power. And retaliatory tariffs by other countries could nullify terms-of-trade gains. Thus – not for the first time – a neat theory turns out to have limited practical relevance. See Irwin, op. cit., pp. 106–15.
19 World Bank, *Global Economic Prospects 2005: Trade, Regionalism and Development*, World Bank, Washington, DC, 2004.

b) Multilateral liberalisation

The rationale for liberalisation through 'multilateral reciprocity' is that unilateral liberalisation is politically difficult in late 20th- and early 21st-century conditions of democratic politics and strong interest-group activity. GATT and WTO negotiations help to contain protectionist interests and mobilise exporting interests; and multilateral agreements provide fair, non-discriminatory rules for all.

Multilateral liberalisation was successful during the GATT when the latter had a relatively slim agenda, club-like decision-making dominated by a handful of developed countries (especially the USA and the EU), and the glue of cold war alliance politics. It has proved spectacularly unsuccessful in the WTO, given its large, unwieldy agenda, chaotic UN-style decision-making in a vastly expanded membership, and without the glue of military alliances after the cold war. Deadlock in the Doha Round probably shows that future multilateral liberalisation will be modest at best and could well prove elusive. Arguably, the best the WTO can hope for is to lock in pre-existing unilateral liberalisation through binding commitments, and gradually improve the functioning of non-discriminatory multilateral rules. Even that will be a tall order, given the parlous state of the WTO. There is every prospect that multilateral trade rules will be undermined by major players seeking to evade them, with extra pressure coming from proliferating, discriminatory bilateral and regional trade agreements. Weaker multilateral rules will be a much bigger cost for developing countries than the extra multilateral liberalisation forgone as a result of Doha Round failure.

c) Bilateral and regional liberalisation

Proponents argue that small clubs of like-minded members can take liberalisation and rules faster, wider and deeper than in the WTO, and act as 'building blocks' to further multilateral liberalisation and rule-making. Sceptics say they are 'stumbling blocks', diverting attention from the WTO, creating 'spaghetti bowls' of discriminatory trade restrictions, and generally favouring powerful players at the expense of the weak.

The reality is mixed. Non-discriminatory unilateral and multilateral liberalisation blunt the damaging effects of discriminatory trade agreements. There is little prospect of the world economy retreating to the warring trade blocs of the 1930s. Strong, 'WTO-plus' FTAs can also make sense in certain circumstances. But the record in developing-country regions is not encouraging. Latin America and Africa have a messy patchwork of weak FTAs that do not liberalise much trade or improve upon WTO rules, but do create complications, especially through trade-restricting rules of origin, and divert attention both from the WTO and from unilateral reforms. This is also the emerging picture of FTAs in East and South Asia.

d) The role of donors[20]

Foreign aid, with conditions attached by the IMF, the World Bank and other donors, has clearly played a big part in driving Washington Consensus-type reforms in many developing countries. This has gone way beyond developing countries' (relatively

---

20   This section draws on Fredrik Erixon and Razeen Sally, 'Trade and aid: countering New Millennium Collectivism', *Australian Economic Review*, 39(1), 2006, pp. 69–77.

weak) liberalising commitments in the WTO and FTAs. Arguably, unilateral liberalisation has not been truly 'unilateral' when it has depended on donor policy preferences and aid with strings attached. The record of IMF stabilisation packages and World Bank structural adjustment packages has been mixed at best, and certainly disappointing compared with optimistic expectations in the 1980s.[21] Often donor-driven reforms have proceeded in stops and starts, with reversals en route. Projected growth and poverty-alleviation effects have not materialised. The politics of aid is even more dubious than its economics. 'Conditionality' is empty rhetoric when self-serving interests at both ends of the pipeline ensure that aid continues to flow, even when promised reforms are not delivered. And the perception that Western donors are imposing reforms on otherwise reluctant countries is hardly sustainable: local 'ownership' is lacking (to borrow aid jargon), and it invites a backlash and reform reversal at home.[22]

The bottom line is that countries that have seen strong, sustained, unilateral liberalising reforms are those whose governments have driven reforms ('from below', as it were) rather than having them imposed by donors ('from above'). Aid at its best has smoothed short-term adjustments; and donor conditionality has provided a 'good housekeeping seal of approval' – an international signal of reform credibility – more than anything else. In these countries (most in East Asia and eastern Europe, and a few in Latin America), aid has not been central to reform success. Where there has been more reliance on aid and donor

---

21   World Bank, *Assessing Aid: What Works, What Doesn't, and Why*, Oxford University Press, Oxford, 1998; World Bank, *1998 Annual Review of Development Effectiveness*, World Bank Operations Evaluation Department, Washington, DC, 1998.

22   P. T. Bauer, 'Foreign aid: abiding issues', in Bauer, *From Subsistence to Exchange and Other Essays*, op. cit.

conditionality, reforms have a far worse record. This applies to Africa in particular.

Seen in this light, the new conventional wisdom on aid is wrong-headed and dangerous. The UN Millennium Project and the Africa Commission Report both propose to double or even triple aid between 2005 and 2015, particularly with Africa in mind. The UN idea – or rather, Jeffrey Sachs's idea – is a new version of the old principle of aid: poor countries lack resources to invest, and donors have to fill this 'financing gap' with a 'big push' of investment if growth is ever to occur.[23] A sudden and massive increase in aid threatens to repeat past mistakes and provide extra incentives to delay and derail, not promote, market-based reforms. Available evidence shows that aid does not improve the productivity of investment; it diverts funds to stimulate government consumption and current spending; it has a negative impact on domestic savings; and, by expanding the role of already dysfunctional governments, it breeds waste and corruption. In short, this approach is misguided top-down intervention.[24]

A softer version of aid optimism, associated with the World Bank, assumes that countries are poor because of bad policy choices and weak institutions, and that aid can lock in already accomplished reforms and facilitate additional reforms.[25] This view is politically naive, though a convenient fiction for elites who profit from the aid business. The main objection is that aid has not and probably will not be a good midwife to market-based reforms. On the contrary, aid is given more often than not to support failed

23   UN Millennium Project, *Investing in Development: A Practical Plan to Achieve the Millennium Development Goals*, Earthscan, New York, 2005; Sachs, op. cit.

24   William Easterly, *The White Man's Burden: Why the West's Efforts to Aid the Rest Have Done So Much Ill and So Little Good*, Penguin, New York, 2006.

25   World Bank, *Assessing Aid*, op. cit.

policies; and there is a high incidence of repeat lending to governments without a good track record of market-based reforms.

A particular version of the aid-to-reform idea is the 'aid-for-trade' scheme that is now discussed in the Doha Round. No one has yet defined its *modus operandi*. Is it a structural adjustment programme, an unemployment insurance programme, a budget support programme, an industrial promotion programme, or something else? Whatever the purpose, the history of aid warns us of the perils of such a scheme. A basic problem with the idea is that countries should be protected from the market-based structural adjustment that trade liberalisation entails. That is in direct conflict with the reality of development.

e) Preliminary summary

Strong reforming countries have relied overwhelmingly on unilateral liberalisation. This has sometimes translated into stronger multilateral commitments and more flexible, pragmatic participation in the WTO. China and Vietnam are the textbook examples. But further substantial liberalisation through trade negotiations, whether in the WTO or through FTAs, is unlikely. Finally, aid-induced liberalisation has not really worked: its political economy is highly dubious. Hence it is a mistake to rely even more on aid for further market-based reforms.

What lessons for future liberalisation?

As we have seen, the conditions for further liberalisation and associated structural reforms are more difficult today than they were in the heyday of the Washington Consensus. Reform complacency results from a post-crisis environment of buoyant growth and normal interest-group politics. There is dissatisfaction with previous reforms in parts of the developing world. Some anti-liberalisation ideas are enjoying a minor revival. Lastly, the politics of 'second-generation' trade-policy reforms is proving much more difficult than that of 'first-generation' reforms. The latter involve the reduction and removal of border barriers. This is relatively simple technically and can be done quickly – though politically these measures are rarely easy. The former are all about complex domestic (though trade-related) regulation, such as services regulation, regulation of food-safety and technical standards, intellectual-property protection, public procurement, customs administration and competition rules. These reforms are technically and administratively difficult, and take time to implement. They demand a minimum of capacity across government, especially for implementation and enforcement. Above all, they are politically very sensitive, as they affect entrenched interests that are extremely difficult to dislodge.

Still, there is a strong case for further market-based reforms in general, and for external liberalisation in particular. Reduction of what are still high barriers to trade, foreign investment and the cross-border movement of people holds out the promise of higher growth, and significant poverty reduction and improvements in human welfare. Stalled reforms and reform reversal threaten to deprive hundreds of millions of people of the life-chances they deserve. These are the stakes. Against this backdrop, the following challenges lie ahead:

First-division reformers

First-division reformers are the 20–25 developing countries – the 'new globalisers' – that have already gone far with macroeconomic stabilisation, and internal and external liberalisation. They have plugged themselves into globalisation. Their task is to go farther with dismantling border barriers to trade and opening the door to FDI. But their bigger challenge is to make much more progress on trade-related domestic reforms – the 'structural' and 'institutional' reforms where progress to date has been too slow. This entails tackling the second-generation issues mentioned above. What is needed is a culture of permanent, incremental reforms, mainly of the second-generation variety, that build on the foundations of first-generation reforms, so that the economy adapts flexibly to changing global conditions. That is easier said than done. The great difficulty lies in doing serious reforms in conditions of normal interest-group politics, without an economic crisis to concentrate minds. But the alternative is creeping sclerosis in times of plenty, and excessive reliance on a crisis for the next reform wave.[26] That cannot be good for long-term political, social and economic health.

Such are the broad trade-policy priorities for first-division developing countries. In this context, the following points deserve emphasis.

First, there needs to be a clearer link between trade policy, on the one hand, and *domestic* economic-policy and institutional reforms, on the other. Trade policy should be coupled strongly

---

26 Mancur Olson, *The Rise and Decline of Nations: Economic Growth, Stagflation and Social Rigidities*, Yale University Press, New Haven, CT, 1982; Organisation of Economic Cooperation and Development, *Economic Policy Reforms: Going for Growth*, OECD, Paris, 2007.

with competition-friendly measures to improve the domestic business climate. It should be better hitched to domestic reforms. For example, there should be ways of linking trade and FDI liberalisation, and trade-related regulatory reform, to measures to shorten and simplify regulations that hinder business at home. Such red tape includes procedural hurdles that have to be overcome before starting a business, obtaining licences, registering property, getting access to credit, employing workers, paying taxes, protecting investors and filing for bankruptcy. Red tape directly affecting exports and imports includes the documentation, time taken and costs of clearing goods through customs. These regulations are documented, classified and ranked in the World Bank's annual *Doing Business* report. Second-generation trade-policy reforms also depend on the quality of public administration and the rule of law (i.e. the quality of the legal framework governing property rights and contracts, and their enforcement by the judicial system). These relate to some of the World Bank's governance indicators and cross-country rankings.[27]

Second, and following directly from the previous point, trade policy should be seen less through the prism of trade negotiations and international organisations, and (as argued above) more through the prism of the domestic economy. Second-generation reforms in particular are bundled up with domestic politics and economics; initiating and implementing them is overwhelmingly a domestic affair; and the scope for productive international negotiations and solutions is restricted. That is already becoming evident with the regulation of services trade and trade-related product standards, and of policies towards inward investment.

---

27 World Bank, *Doing Business in 2007*, op. cit.; World Bank governance indicators, *www.worldbank.org*.

It will become even more evident as global production networks and the movement of people across borders bite ever deeper into domestic institutions.

As trade policy becomes evermore entwined with domestic policies and institutions, it follows that there should be more reliance on unilateral measures, including external liberalisation, and correspondingly less reliance on reciprocal liberalisation through the WTO and FTAs. Unilateral reforms should then be locked in through stronger WTO commitments. This should be the foundation for advancing national market-access and rule-making interests in the WTO. Governments should also exercise caution with FTAs, avoiding quick and dirty ones and engaging only in those that are comprehensive, WTO-plus and clearly linked to competition-enhancing domestic reforms.

Third, there should be much more policy *transparency*. Trade policymaking is usually opaque. Too little is known and understood about the effects of different combinations of trade policies. Consequently, public discussion of policy choices is usually uninformed and misguided. One should add that this applies almost as much to developed countries as to developing countries. For example, anti-dumping and rules-of-origin procedures in the EU are shrouded in secretive, discretionary and ultimately arbitrary behaviour, with restricted external access to information.

What is lacking is what Patrick Messerlin calls a 'culture of evaluation'.[28] Independent think tanks and even government bodies should do much more detailed research and analysis on the costs and benefits of trade policies in different sectors of the economy, and then disseminate findings to the public. This would

---

28 Patrick Messerlin, *Europe After the 'No' Votes: Mapping a New Economic Path*, Institute of Economic Affairs, London, 2006.

facilitate more informed, intelligent public discussion of policy choices.[29] One model to examine is that of the Australian Productivity Commission (formerly the Tariff Board). This is a governmental body, but it is independent and has statutory powers. It provides research and analysis on trade-related issues in Australia; and its conclusions do make their way into the public debate. The Tariff Board's groundbreaking work did much to reveal the costs of protection to the Australian public back in the 1970s, at a time when Australia was a highly protected economy. This generated much public discussion at the time, and in many ways prepared the ground for the radical opening of the Australian economy in the 1980s. Such 'transparency boards' could be set up at relatively low cost in developing countries.

Taken together, these reform priorities are as much about *simplicity* and *transparency* as they are about *liberalisation*. The case for transparency has been made above. Simplicity is all about making complex bureaucratic procedures shorter, more predictable, and also more transparent. This would lessen the costs of doing business – for domestic *and* foreign traders and investors. Hence the importance of linking trade policy to nitty-gritty domestic reforms.

Fundamentally, these reforms boil down to restructuring the state, away from the large overactive state that intervenes badly across the range of economic activity, and towards the limited state that performs a smaller number of core functions well. The latter should focus on providing and enforcing a framework of rules for market-based competition. To use Michael Oakeshott's

---

29   This is the headline objective of the European Centre for International Political Economy (ECIPE), the new Brussels-based think tank I run with Fredrik Erixon. See our mission statement at *www.ecipe.org*.

distinction, the state should be an 'umpire' of a 'civic association', not an 'estate manager' of an 'enterprise association'.

Lower-division reformers

Lower-division reformers are overwhelmingly in the low-income and least-developed bracket and have higher border barriers than first-division reformers in addition to bigger domestic obstacles to trade and investment. They are less globalised. Their first priority should be to reduce border barriers and simple non-border barriers (such as some red-tape procedures that give them low rankings in the World Bank's *Doing Business* report). They have less capacity than first-division reformers for implementing more complex second-generation reforms. These could wait until the easier reforms are done. The real dilemma is that countries at the bottom of this pile, especially among the least-developed countries, are mired in political instability and civil strife, with failed and failing states that do not perform the most basic public functions. Such countries do not have the capacity to implement even simple reforms. Aid-driven solutions have failed, but what is the substitute?

All countries face reform complacency and fatigue. But labour-abundant countries that have inserted themselves into global production networks are most likely to have interest-group coalitions and institutions to defend existing open-market reforms and promote further reforms. Resource-abundant countries have a weaker political-economy base. They are more likely to let reforms lapse and squander the rents from commodity booms. They are doubly challenged in building coalitions of interests to keep reforms going, and to strengthen institutions so that wealth is both generated sustainably and spread widely.

Several other policy challenges come to mind, all directly or indirectly related to trade policy. Here is a brief list, with equally brief answers.

1) How should trade-policy reforms be sequenced with other reforms, such as those relating to macroeconomic policy? Should reforms be fast or gradual?

There are no general answers to these questions. They depend on circumstances, and expediency will dictate different answers in different places at different times. What matters more is the general thrust: a medium-to-long-term commitment to liberalise in the direction of a market-based, globally integrated economy.

2) What is the link with political systems? Is democracy or authoritarianism better suited to market-based policy reform? Do such reforms have a better chance under right-wing or left-wing governments?

Again, there are no general answers. For every example to support one thesis, there is a counter-example to support the opposite thesis. Reforms have succeeded in widely differing political systems, and under governments of different political hues, just as they have failed across the spectrum of political systems and partisan politics.

3) What role is there for industrial policy?

There is leeway for experimentation, adapted to different local conditions. Economy-wide measures, such as improving transport and communications infrastructure, as well as education and skills, can dovetail with trade and wider economic-policy reforms.

So can other 'soft' measures such as trade and investment promotion through information dissemination, organising trade fairs and the like. But selective promotion and protection of chosen industries has a questionable record; and 'hard' industrial policy of the picking-winners variety has an abysmal record: it should be avoided.

4) What about social policies?
Are social safety nets needed alongside liberalising reforms? How generous should they be? Should 'losers' be compensated?

These questions of distribution and equity elicit quite different responses. The classical-liberal response is to keep government limited, focused on its role to provide and enforce a framework of rules for an open, competitive market economy. Basic social safety nets should be provided where affordable. Beyond that, the classical liberal has little interest in redistribution. In contrast, the social-democratic response is to give high priority to redistribution, with government playing an active role.

These debates have taken place mostly in developed countries, but they are of course relevant to developing countries. On the one hand, developing countries have less financial scope for redistribution compared with developed countries. They also have bigger institutional constraints. Ambitious social policies risk scattering scarce resources that should be focused on liberalising reforms. On the other hand, big and widening differences between income groups and regions could undermine popular acceptance of core reforms.

Here also there are no easy, general blueprints. There is room for experimentation and trial-and-error learning. But one thing is needed: better *delivery* of existing public services, including the provision of social-safety nets. These are the last bastions of the command economy. Administrative mechanisms squander public funds and fail to serve those most in need. More market mechanisms are needed, including competition from private-sector suppliers of services. That also opens up possibilities for trade, FDI and cross-border labour movement in traditional public services such as healthcare, education and the utilities, and even beyond to cover housing, social security and pensions. These 'third-generation' reforms are the next frontier.

Conclusion

The naysayers, from the hard and soft left, and the conservative right, hold that liberalisation has not delivered the goods. They argue for various forms of government intervention, at national and international levels, to tame 'market fundamentalism' and 'neoliberal globalisation'. Interventionist ideas on trade (and aid) are not new; they hark back to pre-Adam Smith, 'pre-analytic' mercantilism (as Schumpeter called it). What they have in common is an age-old distrust of markets and faith in government intervention – what David Henderson calls 'New Millennium Collectivism'.[30] Such collectivist thinking is on the rise again. But it is still wrong and dangerous. It glosses over the damage done by interventionist policies in the past, and misreads the recent and historical evidence. The latter shows that external liberalisation, as part of broad market-based reforms, has worked: countries that have become more open to the world economy have grown faster

30 On the provenance and progress of these ideas, see David Henderson, *Anti-Liberalism 2000: The Rise of New Millennium Collectivism*, Institute of Economic Affairs, London, 2001.

and become richer than those that have opened up less or which have remained closed.

There is much unfinished business. Barriers to trade, and the cross-border movement of capital and people, remain high: indeed, more so in developing countries than in developed countries. But a combination of material circumstances and changes in the climate of ideas makes market-based reforms more difficult now than was the case a decade ago. The stakes, however, are too important for reform challenges to be avoided. While there is no imminent threat of global economic collapse, stalled reforms threaten to slow down globalisation's advance, thereby depriving the world's least-advantaged people of the life-chances that globalisation offers. That would reinforce strong pressures, from an alliance of old-style protectionist interests and new-style ideological forces, for overactive government to restrict economic freedom and the operation of the market economy. That is why new-old collectivist ideas need to be countered with full force.

Thus it falls to free trade's friends to make a strong case for further reforms, including external liberalisation, and practically go about assembling reform coalitions. To borrow J. S. Mill's felicitous phrase again, they should spread their word *in season with* global political currents, anti-protectionist producer and consumer interests, and (often unanticipated) events.

4 THE WORLD TRADE ORGANIZATION

The great political virtue of multilateralism, far exceeding in importance its economic virtues, is that it makes it economically possible for most countries, even if small, poor and weak, to live in freedom and with chances of prosperity without having to come to special terms with some Great Power.

JACOB VINER

In recent years, the impression has often been given of a vehicle with a proliferation of backseat drivers, each seeking a different destination, with no map and no intention of asking the way.

THE SUTHERLAND REPORT

The quotes above signify the highs and lows of the WTO. Its establishment in 1995 was hailed as a significant strengthening of multilateral trade rules. This was supposed to transform a 'power-based' trading system into a 'rules-based' one, protecting the small and vulnerable from the predation of the big and powerful. It gave flesh, blood and, above all, legal expression to the founding spirit of the GATT that Jacob Viner wrote about a half-century earlier. Prevailing winds outside Geneva were also blowing favourably: liberalisation was in the air almost everywhere, in the OECD, the developing world, and in the ex-command economies.

A little more than a decade later, the Doha Round seems to

be at a perpetual stalemate and on the verge of collapse. It listed heavily from the start, and several attempts to right it have failed. As the Sutherland Report indicates, the WTO seems immovable: it is full of cacophonous navigators without a compass, steering wildly in all sorts of vague and contradictory directions. Outside Geneva, the winds of liberalisation have subsided, there are counter-currents buffeting market-based reforms, and governments seem keener to negotiate a hotchpotch of PTAs than to do serious business in the WTO.

How has this come to pass? And what is the future of the WTO after the Doha Round? Is it capable of upholding multilateral rules for open international trade? Can it help to secure and extend the global market economy? Or is it a lost cause, crippled by anti-market forces within and without?

From GATT to WTO

The trade economist's textbook argument is that unilateral liberalisation is the 'first-best' method to open the national economy to external competition. But, given the realities of modern politics – interest-group lobbying for protection; ingrained mercantilist thinking; the perception that liberalisation hurts the poor and vulnerable – this is difficult to achieve in practice: hence the merit of the 'multilateral reciprocity' that the GATT/WTO embodies. The following advantages come to mind:

- Inter-governmental negotiations and binding international obligations help protect governments against powerful protectionist interests at home, and mobilise the support of domestic exporters.

- WTO rules provide rights to market access for exports; and rights against the arbitrary protection and predation of more powerful players. This is particularly important for developing countries.
- Multilateral rules can bolster domestic reforms and reinforce their credibility with exporters, importers, local and foreign investors, and, not least, consumers. This is another way of saying that the WTO, at its best, is a helpful auxiliary to good national governance.

This standard *raison d'être* was easier said in the old GATT than done in the WTO. In many ways the WTO is the victim of its own success; of the successful conclusion of the Uruguay Round and the huge transition from the GATT to the WTO. Six underlying trends need to be highlighted, all of which ring alarm bells:

1) The Uruguay Round agreements not only take the WTO wider, with broader sectoral coverage; they also go much deeper into domestic regulation than previous GATT agreements. Understandably so: if the WTO disregarded domestic regulatory barriers, lower protection at the border would be nullified by higher protection behind it. Hence the need for procedural disciplines on regulations of services, subsidies, food-safety and technical standards, customs valuation, and much else that is 'trade-related'. A common minimum-standards approach to domestic regulation can, however, lead to regulatory overload. The biggest danger is a creeping standards-harmonisation agenda. Detailed, prescriptive regulations are intended (at least implicitly) to bring developing-country standards up to developed-country

norms. The TRIPS (Trade Related Intellectual Property Rights) agreement on intellectual property – the most regulation-heavy of all Uruguay Round agreements – sets the precedent for pressure to harmonise labour, environmental, food-safety and other product standards. This 'intrusionism' in the domestic policies and institutions of the developing world is noxious: economically, it can raise developing countries' costs out of line with comparative advantage and has a chilling effect on labour-intensive exports; politically, it goes too far in curtailing national regulatory autonomy.[1]

2) The GATT reciprocity model effectively tackled border barriers that are relatively easy to quantify, compare and bargain over. Trade policy today, in contrast, encompasses complex, opaque domestic regulations on all manner of trade-related issues for which data are lacking and comparison more subjective. These 'second-generation' issues are intimately bound up with local institutional particularities, administratively demanding and politically very sensitive. They are less amenable to reciprocal bargaining and one-size-fits-all international rules than is the case with relatively simple tariffs and quotas. That makes progress in the WTO elusive.

3) The legalisation of the WTO is double-edged. Dispute settlement is much stronger than it was in the GATT: it has acquired legal teeth and bite. And it has worked rather well: increasing numbers of developed and developing countries have used it; and compliance has generally been good. Given the quasi-automatic nature of the mechanisms, however, governments have more incentive to fill in regulatory gaps in

---

1   Bhagwati, op. cit., pp. 51–2, 67.

ambiguously worded WTO agreements through litigation –
especially when diplomacy and negotiations are not working.
This is a dangerous and slippery slope. A large, diverse
gathering of sovereign nations such as the WTO, with at
best a brittle political consensus, must make collective policy
choices through diplomacy and negotiation, not by default
through dispute settlement. The Dispute Settlement Body
simply does not enjoy the political consensus or legitimacy to
'create' law as a means of driving policy.[2]

4) The WTO is increasingly politicised. Externally, it faces the
brunt of the anti-globalisation backlash, and is rocked by a
combination of old-style protectionist interests and new-style
NGOs. Even more vexing are its deeper internal fissures. The
vast expansion of membership since the late 1980s (see Figure
8) has added new sets of developing-country interests and
preferences; and it has made decision-making more unwieldy
and snail-like. Day-by-day, the WTO has become more like
the UN. Windy rhetoric, adversarial point-scoring, political
grandstanding and procedural nit-picking seem to have
substituted for serious decision-making. The GATT escaped
these pitfalls because it had a reasonably clear purpose, a
relatively slimline negotiating agenda and intimate, club-like
decision-making among a handful of key players. The WTO,
sadly, has degenerated into a talking shop reminiscent of the
UN General Assembly.

5) The accelerating spread of discriminatory bilateral and
regional trade agreements seems to be pre-programmed,
not least in reaction to stalled multilateral liberalisation.

2   Claude Barfield, *Free Trade, Sovereignty, Democracy: The Future of the World Trade
Organization*, American Enterprise Institute, Washington, DC, 2001.

Figure 8   WTO Members; countries that had signed the GATT

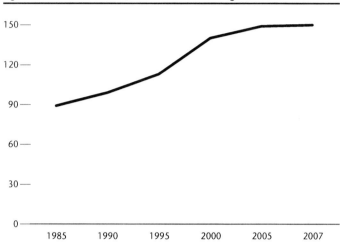

Note: Countries having signed GATT 1985–1990 and countries having entered the WTO 1995–2007
Source: WTO: http://www.wto.org/english/thewto_e/whatis_e/tif_e/org6_e.htm;
http://www.wto.org/english/thewto_e/gattmem_e.htm

PTAs are not uniformly bad, but they do lead to a 'spaghetti bowl' of discrimination and red tape in international trade, driven by power politics. This is precisely what GATT-style multilateralism was supposed to contain and reduce. PTAs also risk diverting political attention and negotiating resources away from the WTO. This will be covered further in the next chapter.

6) The 'high politics' of foreign policy matters for the 'low politics' of trade policy. The GATT was founded in the early stages of the cold war; and the Western alliance held it together during the cold war. That glue has since dissolved. In particular, the USA and western Europe lack the strategic

bonds of a shared security policy to bridge differences and forge common positions in trade negotiations.

Taken together, these pressures have virtually crippled the old GATT's traditional strength: its ability to deliver results through effective diplomacy and negotiation. A wider and more intrusive regulatory agenda makes it more difficult to maintain political legitimacy with governments and interest groups (now including NGOs). It has also blurred the WTO's focus and made it drift towards multiple and contradictory objectives. It has become painfully difficult to make the GATT reciprocity model work with the plethora of non-border issues on the WTO's agenda. Stalled negotiations increase the temptation to settle sensitive policy dilemmas through adversarial litigation, which further tests the political legitimacy of the system. The hyperinflation of member-ship, with the attendant desire to widen the decision-making circle and make it more inclusive and participatory, strains the workability of the system to its limits. And, lastly, the unifying glue of the cold war has dissolved. For these reasons, the WTO as a *negotiating* mechanism has not really functioned since the late 1990s.

The Doha Round

WTO members tried to launch a new 'Millennium Round' of trade negotiations, but failed spectacularly at the disastrous Seattle Ministerial Conference in late 1999. A new round was launched at the Doha Ministerial Conference in November 2001 – but thanks only to September 11th, and the subsequent perception of global political and economic crisis. Hence the 'Doha Development

Agenda' – the official title of the round – merits the sobriquet 'the Bin Laden Round'.

WTO members agreed to a large, complex and ambitious agenda, with 21 subjects dealt with in eight negotiating groups. There was a market-access core, i.e. negotiations on further trade liberalisation, as demanded by the USA, the Cairns Group (of leading developed- and developing-country agricultural exporters), and a few others. Developing countries demanded the inclusion of the 'implementation agenda' (flexibility and assistance in implementing Uruguay Round agreements), flexibility in interpreting WTO rules on patent protection and, more generically, a reconsideration of Special and Differential Treatment (S&D – more favourable treatment for developing countries under WTO agreements). The EU managed to get trade-and-environment and the 'Singapore issues' (competition, investment, trade facilitation and transparency in government procurement) included. And there were to be new negotiations on WTO rules (anti-dumping, fisheries subsidies, regional trade agreements and dispute settlement).[3]

Very little progress was made from the start. Ministers were supposed to put a negotiating framework together for the second half of the round at the Fifth Ministerial Conference, held in Cancun in September 2003. This collapsed in all-round acrimony, chaos and farce. Only in July 2004 was such a framework put together. This whittled down a previously large and unwieldy agenda into one focused on the key market-access issues (agriculture, services and non-agricultural goods). Trade facilitation was

---

3 'Ministerial declaration', WT/MIN(01)/DEC/W/1, 14 November 2001; 'Declaration on the TRIPS agreement and public health', WT/MIN(01)/DEC/W/2, 14 November 2001; and 'Implementation-related issues and concerns', WT/MIN(01)/W/10, 14 November 2001. All available at *www.wto.org*.

also included, while the other three Singapore issues were deleted. After that negotiations became deadlocked again.

The following Ministerial Conference, in Hong Kong in December 2005, delivered a pathetic runt of a package: agreement was reached on relatively minor issues (eventual abolition of EU agricultural export subsidies; TRIPS-related decisions concerning developing countries; extension of duty-free and quota-free access to least-developing countries' exports; and 'aid for trade'), while all major policy decisions concerning market access were post-poned.[4] There was little narrowing of differences in subsequent months; and the round was 'suspended indefinitely' in late July 2006. By then there was no real chance of concluding an agree-ment before the supposedly final deadline: the expiry of US Trade Promotion Authority (which the president needs to negotiate and conclude trade agreements) in July 2007. Negotiations formally restarted in February 2007. At the time of writing, they show little sign of breaking the logjam.

What should be achieved? There is still much to do on market access. Direct border barriers to trade remain high in both devel-oped and developing countries. Although the EU and the USA have low average tariffs, they retain high to very high tariffs in agri-culture, textiles and clothing, and other labour-intensive goods – the sectors of major export potential for developing countries. Huge agricultural subsidies in the OECD continue to distort trade. Widespread anti-dumping actions and unreasonably onerous food safety, technical and other standards also have a chilling effect on developing-country exports. Not least, developing countries have

---

4   'Ministerial declaration' and 'Ministerial declaration: annexes', WT/MIN(05)/ DEC, 18 December 2005, *www.wto.org/english/thewto_e/minist_e/min05_e/ final_text_e.htm*.

noticeably higher tariffs and non-tariff barriers than developed countries, and their main effect is to severely restrict imports from other developing countries. (On market-access barriers, see Tables 1 and 2 and Figures 1–5 in Chapter 3.)

A serious Doha Round package would therefore deliver substantially lower developed-country barriers against developing-country exports of agriculture and manufactures; stronger liberalisation commitments by advanced developing countries; stronger developed- and developing-country commitments on trade in services, and some strengthening of WTO rules (e.g. on anti-dumping). More specifically, the EU would have to make further concessions on agricultural market access (tariff reductions and strict limits on exemptions for 'sensitive products'). The USA would have to reciprocate with bigger cuts in domestic farm subsidies. Advanced developing countries, especially Brazil and India, would have to narrow the gap between bound and applied tariffs in agricultural and non-agricultural goods, concede net liberalisation in some products, and restrict the range of 'special products' exempted from agricultural liberalisation. They would also have to make bigger concessions on 'commercial presence' (i.e. foreign investment) in key services sectors. Lastly, developed countries would have to make some concessions on Mode Four in services (cross-border movement of temporary workers).

A big success was never a realistic prospect. Rather, in a climate of all-round defensiveness, most players seemed to converge on a midget of a deal that would have delivered very little net liberalisation. But this foundered on US resistance: it had always insisted on a substantial deal, with significant access to advanced developing-country markets in return for US concessions on farm subsidies and other items.

The apparent collapse of the Doha Round leaves the WTO in very serious trouble. But a midget deal would not make matters better. The widespread perception is that multilateral liberalisation is going nowhere; there will be much greater temptation to unpick existing agreements and flout multilateral rules; many more sensitive cases will be taken to dispute settlement, which will come under greater political strain; action will switch further and decisively to PTAs; and the world trading system will be shaped more by a messy patchwork of PTAs driven by power politics than by fair and balanced multilateral rules.

All the WTO's structural problems described earlier have played into the miserable failure of the Doha Round. This leaves the WTO drifting inexorably in all the wrong directions – towards the easy politics of a UN-style talking shop and a World Bank-style aid agency for developing-country basket cases (through aid-for-trade and other initiatives that have consumed as much attention as market-access negotiations), and ever farther away from the hard politics of liberalisation and the rules that underpin it. Will the collapse of the round concentrate minds among the players who count? Might it induce them to get back to basics, stop the rot and set the WTO on its legs again?

The future of the WTO

Looking beyond the Doha Round, what, if anything, can hold the WTO and the multilateral trading system together? The answer must be to recognise and tackle the WTO's systemic problems – the underlying causes of Doha Round malaise. To get the WTO out of its rut, its members need to do three things: restore focus on a core market-access and rules agenda, i.e. progressive liberalisation of trade barriers, underpinned by transparent, non-discriminatory rules; revive effective decision-making; and, not least, scale back ambitions and expectations.

The WTO agenda

First, a market-access and rules focus would be traditionalist in the sense that it would restore a GATT-like compass to the WTO. But it could not and would not be a return to a golden yesterday. A post-GATT agenda would have to range wider (broader sectoral coverage than the GATT) and venture deeper (procedural disciplines to make trade-related domestic regulations more transparent and non-discriminatory) – but without regulatory overload and a top-down standards-harmonisation agenda. It is a question of finding a balance: one that would have a lowest common denominator of rules and obligations applicable to a critical mass of WTO members, but still one that would allow wide room for national policy and institutional choice. This scenario would be sufficiently open-ended to encourage bottom-up unilateral experimentation in response to local circumstances and challenges. This would in turn promote a decentralised, market-like competitive emulation among governments in search of better practice.

Within this framework, a post-Doha agenda should shift emphasis from liberalisation to rules. The Doha Round has shown that substantial multilateral liberalisation will be elusive in the future. That still leaves other liberalising avenues, notably PTAs and unilateral measures. More important than further multilateral liberalisation is safeguarding multilateral rules for open and stable international commerce. These rules, on tariff and non-tariff measures, at and behind the border, are indispensable. But they are under threat as a result of WTO malfunction. They can be safeguarded and updated only in a multilateral forum, not unilaterally, bilaterally or in regional clubs. Developed countries and advanced developing countries need them to guarantee access to each other's markets. Poorer and weaker developing countries would be squeezed out and further marginalised without them. Given these common stakes, and once the dust of the Doha Round has settled, rules issues should take priority over further multilateral liberalisation.[5]

Decision-making mechanisms

Nothing of substance can be achieved without mending the WTO's broken decision-making mechanism. This does not depend fundamentally on reforming formal procedures: there is no chance of consensus on major internal reforms; and it would be a distraction from more important matters. Rather, effective decision-making depends on inter-governmental political will and *informal* decision-making. This requires recognition of realities outside Geneva. About 50 countries (30 if the EU is counted as one) account for well over 80 per cent of international trade and an even greater share of FDI.[6] This comprises the OECD plus about twenty developing countries that have been globalising rapidly and successfully (most of them in Asia, some in Latin America, and very few in Africa). These are the ones with workable governments, sufficient appreciation of their own interests, negotiating

---

5   This is the gist of a recent thinkpiece by Simon Evenett. See his 'EU commercial policy in a multipolar trading system', Mimeo, 15 February 2007.

6   Counting the EU as one, and stripping out intra-EU trade, ten countries make up about 70 per cent of world trade.

capacity and bargaining power. They need to strike the key liberalising and rule-making deals. They must be active individually and in multi-country coalitions, ranging from informal, broad-based coalitions to smaller, issue-based ones such as the Cairns Group and the G20 on agriculture, and 'Friends Groups' on other issues.

The role of the different players

Within this outer core, there is an inner core of 'big beasts': the USA and EU, of course, but now joined by the increasingly influential developing-country majors, India, China and Brazil. Japan should be there too, but it punches well below its weight in the WTO. The old understanding of an EU–US duopoly driving the GATT/WTO enterprise no longer holds. No doubt the EU will continue to be a WTO heavyweight, and transatlantic cooperation will remain vital. But the EU's leadership credentials are not great. In the WTO, it is too defensive on agriculture and too offensive in trying to push dubious new regulation on environmental standards and other issues. On the wider global stage it cannot surpass the USA, and the rising powers in Asia-Pacific are catching up. More important for the WTO's future will be clearer US leadership, and constructive participation by China, India, Brazil and perhaps Japan. Of the developing-country majors, China's role will be most important. Ultimately, in the absence of leadership by the Big Beasts, nothing in the WTO will move.

These inner and outer cores must concentrate primarily on core market access in agriculture, non-agricultural goods and services, and related core rules (including anti-dumping, safeguards, subsidies, regional trade agreements and dispute settlement). New issues (such as the Singapore issues and trade-and-environment) should be dealt with plurilaterally through opt-ins or opt-outs. This would give developing countries the cushion to join negotiations only if and when they feel ready to do so.

That leaves about a hundred poorer and weaker developing countries – two-thirds of the membership. In Geneva the conventional wisdom is that they can and should participate actively in collective decision-making, with the help of technical assistance and associated 'capacity-building' provided by international organisations and national donors. This is therapeutic multilateralism. It is fanciful, indeed Utopian.

These countries must of course be consulted and will exercise influence through the less developed countries (LDC), African, Caribbean and Pacific countries (ACP), G90 and other 'common-characteristic' groupings. But the plain fact is that they are very marginally involved in the world economy, and most have chronic misgovernment that often descends into ethnic strife, civil war and state collapse. Negotiating resources are also scarce; and there is little ability and political will to implement WTO agreements. Hence these countries are unable to play more than a secondary and reactive role in the WTO. They exercise 'negative' bargaining power, i.e. they can and do block negotiations; but, frankly, they are incapable of exercising much 'positive' bargaining power in the foreseeable future. As is abundantly clear in the Doha Round, they demand entitlements (such as maintenance of their tariff preferences and increased aid) but are not in a position to make credible negotiating proposals of their own.

Providing these countries do not block negotiations, they should be accorded generous old-style Special and Differential Treatment – essentially a free ride. Through Most Favoured Nation (MFN) status, they should have rights to whatever liberalisation is negotiated by others; and preferably duty- and quota-free access to OECD and leading developing-country markets. At the same time, they should not be obliged to reciprocate with their own liberalisation, nor should they be under pressure to sign up to other new obligations if they feel unready to do so. There should be a 'peace clause' on dispute settlement: an understanding that they will not be taken to court, even if in breach of existing obligations. This is not to say, as do most trade NGOs, that continued protection is the right policy for poor countries. Quite the reverse: the main objective should be not to hold up wider liberalisation by those countries that have more weight in international commerce. Others can join when they are ready and willing, i.e. when they come to their senses and see the self-imposed harm done by maintaining protectionist barriers. These terms should not pose a problem for the core group of 50 (or 30). The rest of the WTO membership is of minimal commercial interest and not of significant strategic political interest to the major developed and developing-country powers.

Practical politics dictates that such a two- or multi-tier configuration should not be expressed in formal WTO decision-making procedures. That would be unacceptable to the majority of the membership outside the outer core. It would be needlessly divisive. Rather the key decisions must be taken informally in smaller, self-selecting groups, followed by broader multilateral consultations and some (but not unlimited) diplomatic give-and-take.

More modest ambitions for the WTO

The WTO must adapt to a more modest future. Even with the right dose of realism, there are *narrower* limits and diminishing returns to GATT/WTO-style multilateralism – for the reasons discussed earlier. Post-Doha, market-access and rule-making negotiations should be more cautious and incremental; and trade rounds should probably become a thing of the past. Cautious incrementalism should apply particularly to negotiating further liberalisation, where the political roadblocks are biggest. More priority should be given instead to safeguarding, updating and administering multilateral trade rules. There should be more emphasis on the WTO as an OECD-type forum to share information and ideas, and to improve transparency through mutual policy surveillance, especially for developing countries. Finally, in the absence of a powerful negotiating mechanism, dispute settlement should be exercised with judicial restraint and not extended further. It would be politically illegitimate and counterproductive to advance multilateralism through international public law without an underlying international political consensus. That is just the sort of global-governance hubris to avoid.

A constitution for the WTO?

Finally, let us look at the WTO in a 'constitutional' light. Many call for the WTO, and other international organisations, to become more 'democratic', 'inclusive' and 'participatory'. They argue that participation in decision-making should be open to non-governmental actors, whether from organised business, labour or NGOs. It is argued that wider participation, beyond the confines of an inter-governmental club, is needed to make collective decisions 'legitimate'.[7]

This view reflects an ancient Greek notion of democracy – Benjamin Constant's 'liberty of the ancients'. In modern guise,

---

7   See Daniel Esty, 'The World Trade Organization's legitimacy crisis', *World Trade Review*, 1(1), 2002, pp. 7–22.

the argument is that established political institutions, at national and international levels, are not representative enough: decision-making has to be shared more widely. But it is ahistorical, unempirical, indeed hopelessly naive, to expect masses of individuals in complex societies to make informed collective choices – even in advanced liberal democracies. That is true at the national level. It is even truer of international institutions, far removed from the daily ken and concerns of ordinary people. 'Participatory democracy' would end up giving free rein to the passions and tyranny of the minorities: a cornucopia of well-organised special interests who would hijack political systems and weigh them down with multiple and conflicting objectives.

Many of these organised interests share a profound distrust of the market economy and a faith in government command-and-control mechanisms. That is certainly true of most NGOs swirling around the WTO. Their economically nonsensical arguments against trade liberalisation and associated market-based reforms in developing countries have been a notable feature of the Doha Round. They have forged alliances with the governments of poorer (particularly African) developing countries with scant negotiating resources, and have significantly influenced their defensive, one-sided and ultimately untenable negotiating positions. At Ministerial Conferences, they have encouraged and sometimes orchestrated developing-country blocking tactics. A major fault-line in the WTO is its seemingly limitless indulgence of so-called civil society. It is regrettable that the barbarians have been allowed inside the gates and given licence to vandalise the grounds and wreck the furniture.[8]

---

8   Many of these people are middle-class fakes who flit from conference to workshop around the world presuming to speak on behalf of the poor and oppressed.

Of course, these tendencies derail effective decision-making and liberalisation in the WTO. More fundamentally, they undermine modern constitutional liberalism. The latter's central insight is that democracy has to be checked, balanced and delegated if it is not to trample on the freedom of the individual and degenerate into the tyranny of majorities and minorities. Liberty has to be protected *against* democracy and its offspring of overactive government. This is James Madison's and Alexander Hamilton's legacy to the American republic they helped to found, as embodied in the US constitution and interpreted in *The Federalist Papers*. It applies as much to international politics as it does to national politics. The WTO should be no exception.

The WTO's central objective should be to facilitate the ongoing liberalisation of international commerce with workable rules. That is a libertarian objective, not a democratic one, for it presupposes the protection of individuals' freedom to transact across borders. It also presupposes limited, not open-ended, government. That demands classical liberal-type rules: simple, transparent, non-discriminatory 'negative ordinances' that protect individual property rights *against* government intervention.[9] Within national jurisdictions, such rules are embodied in private (commercial) law. Their external complements are Articles I and

---

Funding from aid agencies, i.e. Western taxpayers, keeps the circus on the road.

9   Classical-liberal-type rules, in the tradition from Hume and Smith to Hayek and Tumlir, are general rules of conduct, applying equally to all, which are negative (or proscriptive) in the sense that they tell actors what not to do, but otherwise leave them free to do as they wish. They should be distinguished from specific, prescriptive regulations, which usually involve executive discretion and fall within the sphere of public administrative law. See Sally, *Classical Liberalism and International Economic Order*, op. cit., pp. 26–8, 115ff.

III of the GATT (on MFN and National Treatment respectively).[10] The point of the old GATT was for governments to collectively tie their hands with rules to limit their interventions and give more sway to the market economy, albeit in a limited policy arena. A 'democratic' WTO would probably go in a different direction. It would be likely to lead to a raft of detailed, prescriptive regulations that would increase government intervention and restrict economic freedom.[11]

Conclusion

The WTO's *raison d'être* is to provide a framework of rules to assist (mainly developing-country) governments that have strategically chosen to take their national economies in a market-oriented, globally integrated direction. That demands willing adherence to WTO rules. The problem with the Doha Round is that it has become home and breeding ground to a swarm of anti-market ideas and activity that defeat the very purpose of the WTO. A majority of developing-country governments, egged on by anti-market NGOs, expect Northern liberalisation while insisting on wholesale exemptions from WTO rules themselves, in addition to their inevitable demands for more aid. Developed-country

---

10   Jan Tumlir, 'International economic order and democratic constitutionalism', *Ordo*, 34, p. 72.

11   As Fareed Zakaria puts it, 'If trade negotiators allowed for constant democratic input, they [WTO agreements] would be riddled with exceptions, caveats, and shields for politically powerful groups ... More democracy in trade policy would mean more policies like agricultural subsidies ... The world has made more economic progress in the last fifty years than in the previous five hundred. Do we really want to destroy the system that made this happen by making it [the WTO] function like the California legislature?' In *The Future of Democracy: Illiberal Democracy at Home and Abroad*, W. W. Norton, New York, 2003, p. 246.

governments are equally to blame for not countering these arguments and for mollifying, instead of confronting, 'civil society', inside and outside the WTO. In essence, they are culpable because they have failed to make the case for global markets and the multilateral rules that strengthen them.

Political realism is also in order – something from which the WTO has taken an extended vacation. The WTO has to work with the grain of global political and economic realities if it is to work at all. That means US leadership, cooperation among major powers, and 'coalitions of the willing' among the approximately fifty WTO members who count. As Martin Wolf says, 'The trick of making multilateral institutions work is to recognise the realities of power, without succumbing entirely to them.'[12] Furthermore, political realism demands future modesty, especially in scaling down ambitions for further multilateral liberalisation, with correspondingly more focus on defending sensible and workable multilateral trade rules. The latter is more important than the former.

Cassandras would conclude that the WTO has already crossed the Rubicon to a permanent state of UN-style infantilism; and that it is incapable of crossing Joseph Conrad's 'shadow line' – from a world of callow irresponsibility to an adult world of real, solid, fixed things. Cautious optimists, on the other hand, would say that with more modest goals and proportionate means in a restricted inter-governmental setting, the WTO might be salvageable. It might just get back to being a helpful auxiliary to national market-based reforms, while avoiding pitfalls ahead, such as the danger of it becoming an EU-style regulatory

12   Wolf, op. cit., p. 295.

agency saddled with an overloaded agenda, or a UN-style development agency disbursing aid and rules carve-outs to developing countries.

5 PREFERENTIAL TRADE AGREEMENTS

We will work with can-do, not won't-do, countries.

ROBERT ZOELLICK

All hat and no cattle.

TEXAN SAYING

Given the parlous state of the WTO, it is not surprising that
governments all over the world have turned to bilateral and
regional negotiations to conclude discriminatory PTAs. These, it
is said, can move faster, wider and deeper than multilateral negotiations. Thus, venting his spleen after the WTO's failed Cancun
Ministerial Conference, Bob Zoellick, the US Special Trade Representative, promised to speed ahead with bilateral deals with
willing 'can-do' partners. Sceptics, on the other hand, say that
PTAs are not what they are cracked up to be. And cynics would
echo the Texanism quoted above.

Do PTAs facilitate regional economic integration, and, by
extension, global economic integration? How credible are negotiating positions, the choice of negotiating partners, and the agreements already in operation? How good or bad is the fit between
PTAs and economic policy at home? And how do they relate to
involvement in the WTO? I will take a look first at general trends

and then at PTAs in Asia, the scene of the most feverish PTA activity in recent years.

Building blocs and stumbling blocs

By July 2005, 330 PTAs had been notified to the GATT/WTO – 206 of them since the establishment of the WTO in 1995 (Figure 9). Over 180 are currently in force, with many more expected to be operational soon. Of the PTAs in force, 84 per cent are free trade agreements (FTAs), with customs unions (CUs) and partial-scope agreements making up the rest.[1] Bilateral (country-to-country) agreements account for over 75 per cent of PTAs in force and almost 90 per cent of those under negotiation. PTA activity has increased quickly since 1999/2000, and even more so since the launch of the Doha Round.[2]

Many regions have long been involved in PTAs. For the EU, this goes back to its beginnings in the European Coal and Steel Community and then the European Economic Community. In North America, it took off with the US–Canada FTA in the late 1980s. Africa, Latin America and South Asia got going in the 1960s; and eastern Europe and the former Soviet Union after the end of the cold war.

---

1   In FTAs members remove tariff and non-tariff barriers between themselves but retain separate trade policies with respect to third countries. Members of a CU have a common external tariff for third-country imports. Partial-scope agreements are between developing countries and have limited product coverage. They are usually notified under the GATT's Enabling Clause. FTAs and CUs are supposed to be comprehensive in scope and conform to the provisions of GATT Article XXIV ('substantially all trade' in goods) and GATS Article V ('substantial sectoral coverage' in services).

2   'Regional trade agreements: facts and figures', *www.wto.org/english/tratop_e/ region_e/regfac_e.htm*; Jo-Ann Crawford and Roberto V. Fiorentino, 'The changing landscape of regional trade agreements', WTO Discussion Paper no. 8, 2005, available at *www.wto.org*.

Figure 9   **PTAs in force, by date of entry**

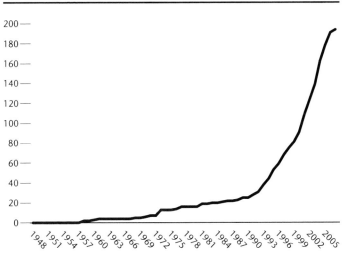

Source: WTO, http://www.wto.org/english/tratop_e/region_e/summary_e.xls

East Asia was the conspicuous exception: it tended to rely more on non-discriminatory unilateral and multilateral liberalisation. Now it is playing catch-up, with PTA initiatives spreading like wildfire in the past six years (Figure 10; see also Figure 11 on the PTA network in the wider Asia-Pacific region). Reform here has mostly taken the form of bilateral FTAs rather than plurilateral or regional negotiations. The major Asian powers – China, India and Japan – are involved, as are South Korea, Australia, New Zealand, Hong Kong, the South-East Asian countries (grouped in ASEAN – the Association of South-East Asian Nations), as well as other South Asian countries. As of 2005, ASEAN as a regional grouping, China and India were involved in seven, nine and

Figure 10 **PTAs in East Asia**

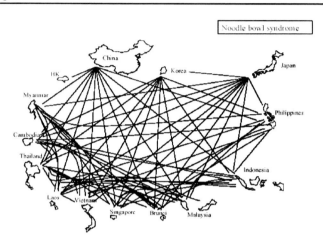

The map shows FTAs signed or under negotiation in January 2006. East Asia is defined here as the 10 ASEANs, China, Japan and Korea.
Source Richard Baldwin 2006: http://www.sussex.ac.uk/Units/caris/T.Carpenter-R.Baldwin-Sussex%20RTA%20Conference-Manage_CEPR_DP.pdf

fifteen FTA agreements or negotiations respectively. If individual ASEAN-member FTA initiatives are counted, there are about 20 FTAs in force and 60 more in the pipeline in China, India and South-East Asia. The USA is involved with individual countries in East Asia, as are some Latin American countries (notably Mexico, Chile and, more recently, Brazil). South Africa is considering initiatives in the region. Of the major powers, only the EU remained outside the fray of PTA activity in Asia – until it changed its policy in late 2006. EU FTA negotiations with India, ASEAN and South Korea started in 2007.[3]

---

3   Rahul Sen, '"New Regionalism" in Asia: a comparative analysis of emerging regional and bilateral trading agreements involving ASEAN, China and India',

Figure 11   **PTAs in Asia-Pacific**

Source: Rahul Sen *ASEAN's Bilateral Preferential Trade and Economic Cooperation Agreements: Evolution, Characteristics and Implications for Economic Integration*, mimeo 2006

Modern economic arguments for and against PTAs spring from Jacob Viner's classic distinction between trade creation and trade diversion. Trade creation results from a shift in production from a high-cost member to a low-cost member of a PTA whereas trade diversion results from a diversion of imports from a low-cost non-member to a high-cost member of a PTA. Now, more complex models examine investment effects, economies of scale and assorted dynamic effects. The political-economy discussion of PTAs revolves around their roles as 'building blocs' or 'stumbling

Journal of World Trade, 40(4), 2006, pp. 553–96; 'The European Union's new trade policy', Special Issue, ed. Simon Evenett, *Aussenwirtschaft*, 61(IV), December 2006.

blocs' to multilateral liberalisation. This has become part of trade-policy Duckspeak.[4]

Why this rush of recent PTA activity?[5] Foreign-policy considerations loom large. PTAs are viewed as a means of cementing stronger political, as well as economic, links with favoured partners. For example, they can be a door-opener to other strategic, security-related agreements. This is clearly the case with Singapore, for example, particularly its FTA with the USA. On the economic front, PTAs are a response to stalled multilateral liberalisation and a weak WTO. Indeed, they are seen as insurance policies against continuing WTO weakness: they secure *preferential* access to major markets and are a means of managing and defusing trade tensions with powerful players.

Not surprisingly, governments tend to present PTAs in a positive light. They are seen as part of a benign 'competitive-liberalisation' process. PTAs among small clubs of like-minded countries can, they argue, take liberalisation and regulatory reform farther than would be the case in a large, heterogeneous and unwieldy WTO. This can, in turn, stimulate multilateral liberalisation.

For PTAs to make economic sense, they should have comprehensive sectoral coverage, be consistent with relevant WTO provisions (in Article XXIV GATT and Article V GATS – General

---

4 A 'duckspeaker' is someone whose speech emerges mechanically from the larynx without engaging the higher brain cells. See George Orwell's *Nineteen Eighty-Four*, in his *The Complete Novels*, Penguin, London, 2000, p. 923.

5 The following account of PTA motives, advantages and disadvantages draws on World Bank, 'Regional trade agreements and development: upside potential and downside risks', Trade Note 24, 13 September 2005, *www.worldbank.org*; World Bank, *Global Economic Prospects 2005: Trade, Regionalism and Development*, World Bank/OUP, Washington, DC, 2004.

Agreement of Trade in Services), and preferably go beyond both WTO commitments and applied practice at home. In other words, they should involve genuine and tangible, not bogus, liberalisation. There should be strong provisions for non-border regulatory cooperation, especially to improve transparency in domestic laws and regulations in order to facilitate market access and boost competition. Rules-of-origin (ROO) requirements should be as simple, generous and harmonised as possible to minimise trade diversion and red tape.[6] Strong, clean 'WTO-plus' PTAs should reinforce domestic economic and institutional reforms to remove market distortions and extend competition. Finally, non-preferential (MFN) tariffs should be low in order to minimise any trade diversion resulting from PTAs.

All this presupposes a sense of economic strategy when entering into PTA negotiations – on choosing negotiating partners, assessing the costs and benefits of negotiating positions, and how they relate to the WTO and to the national economic policy framework. A sense of strategy, with careful preparation through research, analysis and reflection, is even more important for key PTA negotiations and subsequent implementation than it is in the WTO. Bilateral negotiations with major powers – especially with the USA and the EU – are much more issue- and resource-intensive than WTO negotiations. They demand better preparation and coordination across different agencies within government, and between government and non-governmental constituencies, especially business.

---

6   Rules to determine the country of origin of a good do not matter if there are zero tariffs, and matter little if trade takes place on a non-discriminatory (Most Favoured Nation, MFN) basis, as it is supposed to do in the GATT/WTO. But such rules do matter for PTAs, as they determine whether or not a good qualifies for duty-free or preferential-tariff entry to the market of a PTA member.

Unfortunately, the above characterisation is the exception, not the rule, of PTAs in practice. The EU, the North American Free Trade Agreement (NAFTA) and the Australia–New Zealand Closer Economic Relations Trade Agreement (ANZCERTA) are the exceptions. These have zero tariffs and quotas on all (or almost all) intra-PTA goods trade; comprehensive coverage of services trade and of cross-border investment (in goods and services); WTO-plus commitments on cross-border labour movement (essentially free movement of labour in the EU and ANZCERTA); WTO-plus commitments on government procurement, trade facilitation and competition rules; strong disciplines and intensive cooperation on all manner of non-border trade-related regulation; and, not least, low average MFN tariffs that reduce trade diversion.

Most other FTAs and customs unions are weak, however, often falling short of WTO provisions. This is particularly true of South–South PTAs (i.e. between developing countries), but also holds for many North–South PTAs. These tend to be driven by foreign-policy aspirations, but with justifications that are all too often vague, muddled and trivial, having little relevance to commercial realities and the economic nuts and bolts of trade agreements. This can amount to little more than symbolic copycatting of other countries' PTA activity and otherwise empty gesture politics. In such cases economic strategy is conspicuous by its absence.

The predictable results of foreign-policy-driven PTA negotiations are bitty, quick-fix sectoral deals. Politically sensitive sectors in goods and services are carved out, as are crucial areas where progress in the WTO is elusive (especially disciplines on anti-dumping duties and agricultural subsidies). Little progress is usually made in tackling domestic regulatory barriers (e.g. relating to investment, competition, government procurement, trade facilitation, cross-border labour movement, and food-safety and technical standards). These PTAs hardly go beyond WTO commitments, deliver little, if any, net liberalisation and pro-competitive regulatory reform, and get tied up in knots of restrictive, overlapping rules of origin. Especially for developing countries with limited negotiating capacity, resource-intensive PTA negotiations risk diverting political and bureaucratic attention from the WTO and from necessary domestic reforms. Finally, the sway of power politics can result in highly asymmetrical deals, especially when one of the negotiating parties is a major player.

The USA eschews such a 'trade-light' approach, rather advertising strong, comprehensive, WTO-plus FTAs. This normally entails major concessions by its negotiating partners, but few US concessions – as the FTAs now in force with Australia and Singapore demonstrate. US FTAs have wide and deep coverage of goods, services and investment, with strong disciplines to limit domestic regulatory discretion and to improve transparency; very strong intellectual-property protection; mutual recognition agreements on standards and professional qualifications; disciplines on government procurement, trade facilitation and competition rules; provisions for temporary movement of business people; and (fairly weak) commitments on labour and environmental standards. The edifice is underpinned by strong dispute settlement, including investor-state dispute settlement, and mechanisms for intensive regulatory cooperation. On the other hand, there are weaker disciplines or carve-outs for some politically sensitive sectors (particularly in US agriculture); no WTO-plus disciplines on agricultural subsidies or anti-dumping measures; and often complicated and restrictive rules of origin.

Latin America, Africa, the Middle East and the former Soviet

Figure 12   **PTAs in Africa**

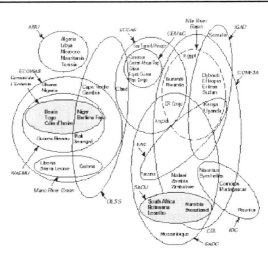

Source: World Bank: Trade Note September 13 2005: http://siteresources.worldbank.org/
INTRANETTRADE/Resources/239054-1126812419270/TradeNote24_Newfarmer.pdf

Union now contain a hotchpotch of weak and partial PTAs. The average African country belongs to four different agreements, and the average Latin American country belongs to seven. (See Figures 12 and 13 for maps of PTAs in the Americas and Africa.) Overlapping PTAs have different tariff schedules, rules of origin and implementation periods. This is exacerbated by poor implementation and relatively high MFN tariffs. The Commonwealth of Independent States, the Common Market of Eastern and Southern Africa (COMESA), the Southern African Development Community, the East African Community, the West African Economic and Monetary Union, and the South Asian Advanced Regional Cooperation Agreement (now the South Asian Free Trade Area)

Figure 13 **PTAs in the Americas**

Source: Inter-American Development Bank: Trade and Cooperation: A Regional Public Goods
Approach: http://www.pecc.org/trade/papers/vancouver-2002/estevadeordal.pdf

are such examples; and they could cost more in lost trade revenues than they gain from tariff preferences.

Restrictive rules of origin are especially troubling. EU, US and NAFTA rules of origin differ considerably from each other, and have different rules for different products (combining two or more criteria in myriad ways). For instance, NAFTA rules of origin may be equivalent to a tariff of 4.3 per cent; and they could be the main factor in the limited impact of NAFTA on Mexican exports. Other PTAs, e.g. the ASEAN Free Trade Area (AFTA), COMESA and the Economic Community of West African States, have less restrictive rules of origin. But nearly all South–South PTAs have significant product-specific exemptions from uniform

ROO criteria, a tendency to increasing product-specific ROO complexity, and high-cost certification procedures to determine the origin of goods.[7]

More generally, complex ROO requirements make no sense in a world where production of goods (and, increasingly, services) is fragmented, with different parts of the value chain located in different countries, and then integrated across borders through trade in components and other intermediate products. Inputs are sourced from many different countries that can supply them at lowest cost. Only then can exports be competitive. Globalisation accelerates this process, but complex ROOs in several, overlapping PTAs throw a spanner in the works. Even subtle differences in rules of origin can raise business costs and divert trade and associated investment. These costs are much more onerous for small and medium-sized trading firms in developing countries than they are for large corporations in developed countries.

Is this PTA 'spaghetti bowl' in danger of being replicated in Asia? Or are the new Asian PTAs more serious? Do they hold out the prospect of strengthening regional and global integration? Now let us look at the PTA activity of the major Asian players: China, the ASEAN countries, India, Japan and South Korea.

---

7 World Trade Organization, *Rules-of-origin regimes in regional trade agreements*, Background survey by the Secretariat, Committee on Regional Trade Agreements, WT/REG/W/45, 5 April 2002, *www.wto.org*; A. Estevadeordal and K. Suominen, 'Rules of origin in the world trading system', Paper prepared for the seminar on regional trade agreements and the WTO, 14 November 2003, *www. wto.org*.

PTAs in Asia[8]

The main players: China, ASEAN, India, Japan, South Korea

China is the driving force for PTAs in Asia. It is considering or negotiating FTAs left, right and centre – in East and South Asia, the Middle East, Latin America, Africa, and with Australia and New Zealand. By 2006, it had nine FTAs on the books and was considering negotiations with up to 30 other countries.

Its core FTA strategy is directed at its close neighbourhood. Politically, China would like to use FTAs to establish leadership credentials in East Asia. On the economic front, strong Chinese FTAs with regional partners might appear to make sense, given ever-closer trade-and-investment linkages in north-east and South-East Asia, particularly involving global manufacturing supply chains. The problem is that the region subsumes a diverse array of economies with big pockets of protection here and there. Opening to trade with China would leave several sheltered sectors exposed to competition. These include agriculture in Japan and South Korea; and agriculture, textiles and clothing in the lesser-developed ASEAN countries (Indonesia, the Philippines, Cambodia, Laos, Vietnam and Myanmar). Extreme agricultural protection in Japan and South Korea will make comprehensive China–Japan and China–Korea FTAs almost impossible to negotiate.

---

8   This section draws on Razeen Sally, 'FTAs and the prospects for regional integration in Asia', ECIPE Working Paper, 1, 2006, *www.ecipe.org/publications/2006/WP'no1_06_Sally.pdf*. Also see Agathe Antkiewicz and John Whalley, 'China's new regional trade agreements', *World Economy*, 28(10), October 2005, pp. 1540, 1554–5; Richard Baldwin, 'Multilateralising regionalism: spaghetti bowls as building blocs on the path to global free trade', *World Economy*, 29(11), 2006, pp. 1451–518; Richard Baldwin, 'Implications of European experiences with regionalism for future economic integration in Asia', Mimeo, 2006; Hadi Soesastro, 'Regional integration in east Asia: achievements and future prospects', *Asian Economic Policy Review*, 1(2), 2006.

The China–ASEAN set of negotiations, more than any other FTA initiative, is the one to watch in the region. The aim is to have an FTA in place by 2010. It would be the largest FTA ever negotiated, covering eleven diverse economies with a population of 1.7 billion and a GDP of US$2 trillion. There has been reasonable progress in eliminating tariffs on trade in goods, but little progress to date has been made on non-tariff barriers in goods, services (where a relatively weak agreement has been reached), investment and other issues. China also has relatively strong, WTO-plus FTAs with Hong Kong and Macau (both admittedly special cases); it has a comprehensive FTA, limited to goods, with Chile; and it is negotiating FTAs with Australia and New Zealand. China is also negotiating, or thinking of negotiating, rather weak FTAs elsewhere in the developing world (for example, with Pakistan, MERCOSUR (Mercato del Sur – Market of the South), the South African Customs Union (SACU) and perhaps India). These are shallow – mostly preferential tariff reductions on a limited range of products.

In all, China is making the running on FTAs in Asia. Its approach is pragmatic and eclectic, ranging from strong (Hong Kong and Macau) to middling-to-weak (probably ASEAN) to very weak (probably India, SACU and other countries in Africa, the Middle East and elsewhere). Even the China–ASEAN FTA is unlikely to create much extra trade and investment if it does not go substantially beyond tariff elimination in goods. Trading interests are placed in the context of foreign-policy 'soft power', i.e. diplomacy and relationship-building. Though China is a little more serious about FTAs than most other regional players, its FTAs are driven more by 'high politics' (competition with Japan to establish leadership credentials in East Asia; securing privileged influence in other regions) than economic strategy. The danger is that this will deliver weak, partial FTAs that create little trade but a lot more political and economic complications. That would send powerful signals to other countries to do the same.

Turning to South-East Asia, Singapore blazed the FTA trail, with Thailand next to follow, and now Malaysia, Indonesia, the Philippines and Vietnam trying to catch up. Singapore has agreements in force with Australia, New Zealand, Japan, the USA, South Korea, India and a host of other minor trading partners; and several others proposed or under negotiation in Africa, the Middle East, South Asia and the Americas. Thailand has agreements in force with Australia, New Zealand, Bahrain, China and India, and one concluded with Japan. It was in negotiations with the USA and others, before the Thai political crisis and the subsequent military coup put all negotiations on hold. Malaysia has an agreement with Japan, and is negotiating with the USA, Australia, New Zealand, India, Pakistan, South Korea and Chile. The Philippines has a new FTA with Japan; Indonesia is negotiating with Japan; and both are looking to start negotiations with others. Vietnam has a bilateral trade agreement with the USA, is negotiating with Japan and considering other negotiations. In addition, ASEAN collectively has negotiations with China, India, Japan, ANZCERTA and South Korea. ASEAN–EU FTA negotiations started in 2007.

Of the ASEAN countries, only Singapore has reasonably strong FTAs, and an especially strong FTA with the USA that has comprehensive coverage and strong rules for goods, services, investment and other issues. But Singapore, with its free-port economy, centralised city-state politics, efficient administration and world-class regulatory standards, is a misleading indicator for the region. Thailand provides a better indicator. Its FTAs were rushed: too many negotiations were launched, and they proceeded too fast, with little overarching strategy. The residual FTA logic was narrowly mercantilist: export-market access in a few sectors was sought in return for import concessions in a few others, while otherwise preserving the domestic-protectionist status quo. This trade-light approach has resulted in weak FTAs that will make little positive difference to competition and efficiency in the Thai economy, but will create complications in the process (not least with a bewildering array of ROO requirements). The US–Thai FTA was likely to be the sole exception owing to US demands for wide and deep commitments. But negotiations ran into serious domestic opposition in Thailand, before being derailed by the Thai political crisis and subsequent military coup.

Thus far most signs point to ASEAN countries becoming entangled in a web of weak and partial FTAs. Many product areas, especially in agriculture, are likely to be excluded from goods liberalisation. Regulatory barriers are unlikely to be tackled with disciplines that go much deeper than existing WTO commitments. Services commitments are unlikely to advance much beyond the WTO's GATS agreement, let alone deliver meaningful net liberalisation or regulatory cooperation (e.g. on mutual recognition of standards and professional qualifications). Provisions on investment and the temporary movement of workers are also likely to be weak, with perhaps even weaker commitments on government procurement, competition rules and customs administration.

More important than all the above considerations, it is already apparent that agreements in force and those being negotiated are creating a 'noodle bowl' of complex and restrictive ROOs. A dog's breakfast of differing general and product-specific ROO criteria is emerging. These differ between bilateral FTAs. Collective ASEAN FTAs with third countries will compound the problem if (as is quite likely) they end up with yet another layer of differing ROO criteria. If this is indeed what emerges, administrative and other compliance costs could be too onerous for most exporters in the region. Many will find it cheaper to pay the MFN-tariff duty. Little trade (and associated FDI) will be created, but there will be more work for customs officials.

India is also newly active with FTAs in its South Asian backyard and in other developing-country regions. In South Asia it has several bilateral FTAs. Hitherto loose regional cooperation is supposed to be transformed into the South Asian FTA (SAFTA) by 2010, leading to a customs union by 2015 and economic union (whatever that means) by 2020. This looks unachievable in practice. For a start, SAFTA excludes Indo-Pakistani trade. Planned negotiations are only on goods: they do not cover services, investment and other non-border market-access issues. There are bound to be plenty of exemptions, given similar trade structures with competing products (especially in agriculture). Finally, severe political problems in the region (the Indo-Pakistani conflict over Kashmir, and the fact that India is completely surrounded by weak, failing or failed states) will make progress very difficult.

India's approach to FTAs outside South Asia is mostly about foreign policy and is trade light, with little economic sense or strategy. An FTA with ASEAN is planned for completion by 2011; and bilateral FTAs are also in place with Thailand and Singapore. ASEAN–India and India–Thailand negotiations have been bedevilled by India's insistence on exempting swathes of products and on very restrictive rules of origin for products covered. In addition, India is part of the BIMSTEC group (the other members being

Bangladesh, Sri Lanka, Nepal, Bhutan, Thailand and Myanmar) that plans an FTA by 2017. It has mini-FTAs – basically limited tariff-concession schemes – in force or planned with several countries and regions, e.g. Chile, SACU, MERCOSUR, IBSA (India, Brazil, South Africa). FTA negotiations have started with the EU, Japan and South Korea.

Japan was the last major trading nation to hold out against discriminatory trade agreements, preferring the non-discriminatory WTO track instead. This has changed decisively in the past five years.

Japan's biggest FTA initiative is the Japan–ASEAN Economic Partnership Agreement, which is supposed to be completed by 2012. It is comprehensive on paper, covering goods, services, investment, trade facilitation and several areas for economic cooperation. Progress has been slow, however – much slower than in the China–ASEAN FTA. This is due to Japanese reluctance to reduce and then phase out agricultural tariffs, and to its insistence on restrictive and often product-specific ROOs, especially for agricultural products (though for some manufacturing products as well). Another complicating factor is that Japan has given greater priority to bilateral FTA negotiations with individual ASEAN countries. Such bilateralism, especially with its noodle-bowl profusion of ROOs, is going to make it very hard to achieve a clean, comprehensive Japan–ASEAN FTA. The latter risks ending up as a loose umbrella for a series of bilateral FTAs.

Japan has several other FTA initiatives in train. It calls its FTAs 'economic partnership agreements' (EPAs) – to indicate that they go beyond traditional FTAs in goods and have comprehensive coverage of trade and investment-related issues in goods and services. That is misleading: EPAs are euphemisms for weak and partial FTAs. In essence, Japan seems to be reacting to China's FTA advance, but without a real strategy.

South Korea is also in the thick of FTA activity. Like Japan, it is defensive on agriculture. Unlike Japan, it seems to be more serious on other negotiating issues. It has made more progress than Japan in FTA negotiations with ASEAN. South Korea and US negotiators concluded an FTA in April 2007. Negotiations with the EU started in 2007.

Regional economic integration initiatives

I will now look at broader regional economic integration initiatives. These are Asia Pacific Economic Cooperation (APEC) and ASEAN; and pan-East Asian and pan-Asian FTA initiatives.

APEC's membership is diverse and unwieldy; its agenda has become impossibly broad and unfocused; its vaunted Open (i.e. non-discriminatory) Regionalism is dead in the water; and these days it is driven by shallow 'conferencitis' and summitry. It cannot be expected to contribute anything serious to regional economic integration. An APEC FTA initiative (FTAAP – Free Trade Area of the Asia Pacific) was launched at the APEC Hanoi summit in 2006.[9] It will go nowhere: political and economic divisions in such a large, heterogeneous grouping are manifold and intractable.

In South-East Asia, the AFTA has an accelerated timetable for intra-ASEAN tariff elimination, but has seen little progress

9   See C. Fred Bergsten, 'Toward a Free Trade Area of the Asia Pacific', Policy Briefs in International Economics no. PB07–2, Peterson Institute for International Economics, February 2007, *www.petersoninstitute.org*.

on 'AFTA-plus' items such as services, investment, non-tariff barriers and mutual recognition and harmonisation of standards. An ASEAN Economic Community, a single market for goods, services, capital and the movement of skilled labour, is supposed to be achieved by 2015. So far, however, ASEAN vision statements and other blueprints have largely failed to remove barriers to commerce in South-East Asia. They seem rather distant from commercial ground realities.

Lastly, there is much talk in the region of folding bilateral and ASEAN FTAs into larger, integrated FTAs that would cover East Asia, and perhaps include South Asia too. An ASEAN Plus Three (APT) FTA (the 'three' being Japan, South Korea and China) has been touted, as has an East Asian FTA that might include Australia and New Zealand. There is talk of a pan-Asian FTA that would include India or SAFTA. Visions of an East Asian Economic Community and even an Asian Economic Community have appeared on the horizon. The first East Asian Summit, held in Kuala Lumpur in November 2005, was supposed to get these bigger regional-integration efforts under way, at least for East Asia.

So far this talk is loose and empty – nothing more. Regional players are speeding ahead with quick and dirty bilateral FTAs, while little progress is being made with the larger ASEAN FTAs (beyond tariff elimination in goods trade). The emerging pattern is of a patchwork of bilateral 'hub-and-spoke' FTAs, in a noodle bowl of trade-restricting rules of origin. This threatens to slow down and distort the advance of regional and global production networks. In particular, it could undermine the dense networks of East Asian production-sharing and trade in manufacturing parts and components ('fragmentation-based trade', or what Richard

Baldwin calls 'Factory Asia'), which are in turn linked to final export markets in Europe and North America.[10] Moreover, such FTA activity distracts attention from further unilateral liberalisation and domestic reforms. That will probably hinder, not help, the cause of regional economic integration.

More generally, bitter nationalist rivalries (especially in northeast Asia and between India and Pakistan), and vast inter-country differences in economic structure, development, policies and institutions, will continue to stymie Asian regional-integration efforts for a long time to come. This applies to East Asia; it applies even more to South Asia.

The implications for Asia in the WTO

Frenetic PTA activity does raise questions about Asian countries' engagement in the WTO and their commitment to the multilateral trading system. Do PTAs reinforce Asian influence in the WTO? Or do they divert attention from it? What impact have they had on Asian participation in the Doha Round?

Some Asian countries were active in the Uruguay Round, though in different ways. India was arch-defensive and led developing-country opposition to developed-country demands. Japan, at the other end, was an active *demandeur* in market-access and rules negotiations. South Korea, Hong Kong, the ASEAN countries, Australia and New Zealand were newly active in the GATT, alongside their general shift to liberal, outward-oriented trade policies and their increasing integration into the world economy.

---

10   Also see Prema-chandra Athukorala, 'Product fragmentation and trade patterns in east Asia', *Asian Economic Papers*, 4(3), 2006, pp. 1–27.

The Doha Round picture looks very different. India has become even more active than it was in the Uruguay Round, but Japan, South Korea and the ASEAN countries have been visibly less active. Most conspicuously, Japan punches well below its economic weight in the WTO. Nearly all East Asian countries have diverted political attention and negotiating resources away from the WTO and towards FTAs. China is the major exception. Its WTO commitments are by far the strongest of any developing country in the WTO (of which more in the next chapter). As a result of its unilateral liberalisation and WTO accession, China's levels of trade protection are low by developing-country standards; and it has acquired a strong stake in a rules-based multilateral trading system. Nevertheless, it has been quiet and low-key in the Doha Round.

The general East Asian neglect of the WTO is extremely myopic, and may prove to be a monumental miscalculation. The region needs an effective WTO. Its integration with the world economy gives it a long-term stake in a liberal trading system underpinned by strong, non-discriminatory rules. A patchwork of overlapping and discriminatory FTAs is not enough; and, in the absence of a healthy multilateral system, will probably be damaging. This logic applies compellingly to South Asian countries too, given their increasing integration into the world economy.

As discussed in the previous chapter, Japan, South Korea, Taiwan, Hong Kong, China, India and the more advanced ASEAN members are in an outer core of about 50 countries (or 30 if the EU is counted as one) that need to be active to restore the WTO's longer-term fortunes. And China, India and perhaps Japan are in an inner core that needs to exercise leadership.

Conclusion

There is now a hearty appetite for PTAs in ever-bigger spaghetti bowls and noodle bowls. It will induce indigestion and worse. But it should not bring on apocalyptic visions of George Orwell's Oceania, Eastasia and Eurasia, each hermetically sealed and at permanent war with the others. The global economy has become too integrated, and new intra-regional and cross-regional PTAs too porous, to turn *Nineteen Eighty-Four* from fiction to reality, or indeed to presage a return to 1930s-style warring trade blocs. That, however, is no excuse for complacency.

Trade policy across the world is now highly unbalanced. It relies too much on (weak and partial) PTAs. This is likely to get worse with the unending stalemate or even collapse of the Doha Round. PTAs are probably not going to tear down the remaining protectionist barriers that matter, whether in North–South or South–South commerce. Nearly all have the hallmarks of trade-light agreements. Some might even come close to being 'trade-free' agreements. A blunt Texan would say that they are 'all hat and no cattle'. As Montaigne said of Seneca's writing, most of these PTAs make 'more sound than sense', and some might even be 'pure wind'. Consequently, PTAs will not be the driving force of regional economic integration or further integration with the global economy. On the contrary, the emerging hub-and-spoke pattern of dirty FTAs threatens to be a force of economic disintegration – especially if the multilateral trading system weakens further.

FTAs are a reality, however; they cannot be wished away; but they can be improved; and they can fit better with trade policy on unilateral and multilateral tracks. That calls for comprehensive, WTO-plus FTAs with simple, harmonised rules of origin.

It is important to 'multilateralise regionalism', e.g. by simplifying and harmonising rules of origin and tariff schedules, and (ideally) making preferences time limited (after which they would be open to all comers on a non-discriminatory basis). If this does not happen, spaghetti bowls and noodle bowls threaten to undermine regional and global production networks.[11] But setting up and operating the requisite regional cooperation mechanisms will prove very difficult, given myriad political and economic divisions in East and South Asia – not to mention other developing-country regions.

Going about FTAs the wrong way – negotiating weak agreements with ROO complications that deflect attention from sensible unilateral reforms and the WTO – could easily lead to a world where most international trade would be governed by power relationships and arbitrary market-distorting preferences. Then the cornerstone of the multilateral trading system, the principle of non-discrimination embodied in the GATT's MFN clause, would become more an abstraction than concrete reality. MFN would end up as LFN (Least Favoured Nation) treatment. This would make a mockery of comparative cost advantages, the foundation of sensible and mutually advantageous globalisation.[12]

---

11 Baldwin, 'Multilateralising regionalism', op. cit.
12 Peter Sutherland et al., *The Future of the WTO: Addressing Institutional Challenges in the New Millennium*, WTO, Geneva, 2005.

6 ASIA, CHINA AND UNILATERAL LIBERALISATION

I trust the government ... will not resume the policy which they and we have found most inconvenient, namely the haggling with foreign countries about reciprocal concessions, instead of taking that independent course which we believe to be conducive to our own interests. ... let us trust that our example, with the proof of practical benefits we derive from it, will at no remote period insure the adoption of the principles on which we have acted ... Let, therefore, our commerce be as free as our institutions. Let us proclaim commerce free, and nation after nation will follow our example.

SIR ROBERT PEEL, ANNOUNCING THE
REPEAL OF THE CORN LAWS,
HOUSE OF COMMONS, 1846

Liberalise first, negotiate later.

MART LAAR,
FORMER PRIME MINISTER OF ESTONIA

It is customary to look first to the WTO, or now to PTAs, or to a combination of the two, to advance the liberalisation of international commerce. This is questionable. As I have argued, the WTO today has severe limitations, as have PTAs. The transition from the GATT to the WTO has narrowed the possibilities for multilateral liberalisation and rule strengthening – as the Doha Round has amply demonstrated. Meanwhile PTAs are unlikely to deliver large doses of additional liberalisation, but will cause extra political and economic complications. Therefore, while trade negotiations have their place, they have distinct limits. Could it be that too much intellectual and political capital is invested in such top-down solutions? Do the solutions lie elsewhere? The quotes above point to a different route: *unilateral* liberalisation by governments *outside* trade negotiations. Hence this chapter begins with the political and economic feasibility of unilateral trade liberalisation in the early 21st century.

The focus then switches to Asia, especially China. Most of Asia slept through the global economic transformations of the last two centuries. That was particularly true of its political and populous giants, China and India. Now they have awoken and are finally integrating into the global economy; and the next half-century will see an Asian transformation of the global economy possibly as profound as that unleashed by the British-led Industrial Revolution. Unilateral liberalisation of trade and foreign investment is central to this dynamic; and China is its driving force. Thus the spotlight here falls on Asian – particularly Chinese – unilateral liberalisation and its implications for trade policy worldwide.

The political economy of unilateral liberalisation

The idea that a reasonably liberal international economic order can be constructed only by international organisations and inter-governmental negotiations is what I have called 'liberalism from above'. It stems from the interwar liberal-idealist tradition and became the established presumption with the post-1945 Bretton

Woods and GATT settlements. Since then it has been given intellectual respectability by the 'liberal-internationalist' tradition in the academic study of international politics. Proponents hold that multiple points of friction between clashing government policies can and do descend into political and economic conflict, including protectionism. Negotiated inter-governmental cooperation in 'international regimes', usually involving international organisations, is necessary to minimise conflict and keep the system open. This requires reciprocity, the exchange of concessions between governments through negotiation, not the 'spontaneous' cooperation of governments unilaterally adapting their policies to changing international conditions. As Robert Axelrod and Robert Keohane put it, 'Co-operation in world politics seems to be attained best not by providing benefits unilaterally to others, but by conditional co-operation.'[1]

This approach was expedient to overcome the political and economic disasters between the two world wars; and to deal with the reality that the USA, unlike nineteenth-century Britain, was unwilling to open its economy unconditionally after 1945. Over time, however, liberalism from above has entrenched a misguided conventional wisdom: namely that international institutions deliver trade liberalisation 'from outside', and only through 'concessions' to foreigners in a game of haggling.

This has become central to the world-view of international bureaucrats and politicians engaged in an endless round of

---

1   Robert Axelrod and Robert O. Keohane, 'Achieving co-operation under anarchy', in David Baldwin (ed.), *Neorealism and Neoliberalism: The Contemporary Debate*, Columbia University Press, New York, 1993, p. 109. Also see Robert O. Keohane, *After Hegemony: Co-operation and Discord in the World Political Economy*, Princeton University Press, Princeton, NJ, 1984; Robert O. Keohane, 'Reciprocity in international relations', *International Organisation*, 40(1), Winter 1986.

conferences and summits. It tends to favour extra regulatory discretion, now at the international level, to intervene here or there, rather than 'negative' international rules to limit government intervention and protect the individual's freedom to transact across national borders. At its extreme, it leads to an unconditional advocacy of international institutions. International cooperation – what is popularly called multilateralism – ends up as incantation and therapy rather than anything with intelligible meaning.[2] To adapt a Bushism, strong advocates consistently mis-overestimate the importance and effectiveness of international institutions, and are blind to their failings, such as excessive, self-serving bureaucracy and misguided meddling. The WTO and its Doha Round are no exceptions. To the 'WTO junkie', trade policy begins and ends in Geneva, and the WTO is the central trade pillar in the architecture of global governance. The Doha Development Agenda has been viewed as a means of delivering development (or salvation) 'from above'. Of such are pipe-dreams made.

Liberalism from above overlooks fundamental lessons from theory, history and the world around us today. Compelling political and economic arguments favour unilateral liberalisation, with governments freeing up international trade and flows of capital and labour independently, not in the first instance via international negotiations. As any student of trade economics knows, welfare gains result directly from *import* liberalisation, which replaces comparatively costly domestic production and reallocates resources more efficiently, and spurs capital accumulation and economies of scale as well as longer-run dynamic gains such as the transfer of technology and skills. Among its many benefits,

---

2   Jan Tumlir, 'Need for an open multilateral trading system', *World Economy*, 6(4), December 1983, p. 400.

import liberalisation provides cheaper inputs and reallocates resources to promising export sectors. Similar and related arguments apply to the liberalisation of inward investment and the cross-border movement of people.

Such gains come more quickly through unconditional liberalisation than through protracted, politicised and bureaucratically cumbersome international negotiations. This Nike strategy ('Just Do It!'), or, to use my alternative catchphrase, 'liberalism from below', can make political sense too. Rather than relying on one-size-fits-all international blueprints, governments have the flexibility to initiate policies and emulate better practice abroad in experimental, trial-and-error fashion, tailored to specific local conditions. In this sense a liberal trade order is not a 'construct' of international negotiations; rather it is *epiphenomenal*, a by-product of unilateral liberalisation by one or several countries, progressively emulated by others.[3] In David Landes's words, it is 'initiated from below and diffused by example'. It induces an open-ended political (or institutional) competition among governments that allows them to spontaneously adjust to each other's practices in a world of uncertainty and flux, and which enables them to adapt to overall change in the world economy in a relatively smooth and efficient manner. It is a dynamic, freewheeling *market-like* process, akin to F. A. Hayek's model of 'competition as a discovery procedure'.

Liberalism from below was the preferred method of the classical economists from Smith to Marshall, and of the titans of mid-Victorian British politics. Britain did indeed lead the way with unilateral trade liberalisation in the second half of the

---

3   Jan Tumlir, 'International economic order and democratic constitutionalism', op. cit., pp. 76–7.

nineteenth century. In 20th- and 21st-century conditions of democratic politics, vigorous interest-group lobbying for protection and ingrained mercantilist thinking, unilateral liberalisation is of course a much more difficult proposition than it was in the nineteenth century: hence the post-1945 logic of reciprocity. Until recently, multilateral reciprocity delivered the bulk of trade liberalisation in the OECD; and regional negotiations served the same purpose within the EU. There were notable exceptions: Ludwig Erhard launched West Germany's domestic and foreign-economic liberalisation unilaterally, which was partially imitated by other western European countries in the 1950s; and Japan, South Korea and Taiwan pursued their selective trade-liberalisation policies unilaterally too.

Since the 1980s there has been a veritable trade-policy revolution outside the West, with region after region shifting from protection and isolation to freer trade and global economic integration. Observers often forget that this has come more 'from below' than 'from above'. The World Bank estimates that, between 1983 and 2003, about 65 per cent of developing-country tariff liberalisation (a 21 per cent cut in average weighted tariffs) has come about unilaterally, with 25 per cent coming from the Uruguay Round agreements and only 10 per cent from PTAs (Figure 14).[4] True, many governments liberalised reluctantly as part of IMF and World Bank structural adjustment programmes. But the strong and sustained liberalisers have gone ahead under their own steam, without the need for much external pressure. That includes several Latin American countries, eastern Europe, the South-East Asian tigers, and now China and India.

---

4   World Bank, 'Regional trade agreements and development: upside potential and downside risks', op. cit., p. 5.

Figure 14 **Share of total tariff reduction, by type of liberalisation 1983–2003**, %

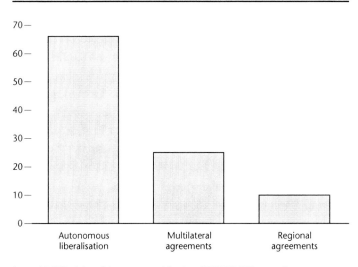

Source: World Bank, http://siteresources.worldbank.org/INTGEP2005/Resources/GEP107053_Ch02.pdf

This brings us to Asia. Modern economic globalisation outside the West is an overwhelmingly Asian phenomenon, and much of it is due to unilateral liberalisation.

The new Asian Drama and the Chinese engine[5]

Gunnar Myrdal's *Asian Drama*, written in the 1960s, painted a bleak picture of Asia at that time and of its prospects.[6] This was

5   This section draws on Razeen Sally, 'Chinese trade policies in wider Asian perspective', op. cit.
6   Gunnar Myrdal, *Asian Drama: An Inquiry into the Poverty of Nations*, Penguin,

apparently a continent hobbled by colonial exploitation, trapped in unequal commercial exchange with the West, and mired in myriad market failures that precluded escape from poverty and progress to prosperity. The conclusion Myrdal and most other development experts drew was that only massive infusions of Western aid, Soviet-style planning and import-substituting protection could overcome market failures and kick-start industrialisation, growth and development. And in a cultural echo from the same period, V. S. Naipaul dismissed India as a 'broken, wounded civilisation'. He could have been referring equally to China after the Great Leap Forward and during the Cultural Revolution.

Today these are popular images of Africa, not Asia (at least East and South Asia). How different the Asian Drama looks now – the exact opposite of Myrdal's diagnosis and prognosis. First Japan, South Korea, Taiwan, Hong Kong and Singapore underwent fast-paced export-oriented industrialisation and catch-up growth as a result of stable macroeconomic policies, domestic competition and opening to the world economy. These policies mattered much more than foreign aid (which in any case tapered off from the late 1950s). The South-East Asian tigers (Malaysia, Thailand, Indonesia and, to a much lesser extent, the Philippines) followed, with large external opening taking place in the 1980s and the first half of the 1990s. The countries of Indochina, notably Vietnam, started opening their borders as part of their transition from Plan to Market from the mid to late 1980s.

China started its opening in 1978, with massive trade-and-investment liberalisation unleashed from the early 1990s. This was crowned by its accession to the WTO, with by far the strongest

Harmondsworth, 1968, three vols.

commitments of any developing country. India's retreat from the 'licence raj' began half-heartedly in the 1980s but a foreign-exchange crisis in 1991 precipitated more radical market-based reforms, including substantial trade and FDI liberalisation.

Of course, the story of Asian policy reforms is more complicated. There were lots of factors at play, not least vast differences between countries in historical legacies, policies and institutions. To varying degrees, and with the exception of free-trade, laissez-faire Hong Kong, government intervention, including industrial policies, import protection and capital controls, coexisted with domestic market-oriented policies and external liberalisation. But two big lessons stand out from a half-century of policy reforms in first East and then South Asia – what is now 'globalising Asia'. First, countries have moved in the direction of the market economy, with better protection of property rights, freer enterprise and competition in place of state ownership and planning, and more exposure to foreign trade and investment. And, second, the market economy has opened up personal freedoms and life-chances – though not necessarily civic and political freedoms – that were unimaginable even a generation or two ago. That is the product of increasing wealth and the institutions that accompany it.

Now let us take a closer look at Asia in the world economy, and then at Asian trade-policy reforms.

Asia and globalisation[7]

Asia was conspicuously absent from the world economy from

7 For an excellent shorthand account of Asia's role in the world economy, see Martin Wolf's columns in the *Financial Times*, e.g. 'Why Europe was the past, the US is the present and a China-dominated Asia the future of the global economy', 22 September 2003; 'Three reasons to be cheerful about the world economy', 30

the Industrial Revolution to relatively recent times (though its decline relative to Europe set in well before the Industrial Revolution). This began to change with the post-1950 rise of Japan and the East Asian tigers, and then changed faster with the opening of first China and then India. The latter two are home to 40 per cent of humanity. With still-low levels of per capita income (China's being 15 per cent and India's 7 per cent of US levels measured at purchasing-power parity) and huge supplies of cheap, productive labour, they have the potential for stellar catch-up growth rates for decades ahead. Their integration into the world economy, still in its early stages, promises to be more momentous than that of Japan and the East Asian tigers, and perhaps on a par with the rise of the USA, Germany and Japan as global economic powers in the late nineteenth century (see Figures 15 and 16 for changing Asian, Japanese, Chinese and Indian shares in world GDP over time).

Japan still dominates Asian economic activity, accounting for over 50 per cent of East and South Asian combined GDP (at market prices). But China is catching up quickly. It is already more globally integrated than Japan in terms of trade and FDI penetration; and has recently displaced Japan as the world's third-largest trading nation in goods. China is ranked fourth in the world for trade in services (if intra-EU trade is excluded). By 2005, trade in goods was 63 per cent of GDP; FDI annual flows were running at over $70 billion and FDI stock stood at over $300 billion (or about 14 per cent of GDP); and multinational

June 2004; 'On the move: Asia's giants take different routes in pursuit of economic greatness', 23 February 2005; 'What India must do to outpace China', 14 February 2006; 'Answer to Asia's rise is not to retreat', 14 March 2006; 'China should stick to trial and error – but risk bolder trials', 7 June 2006.

Figure 15 **Asia's share of global GDP** %
1990, international $m

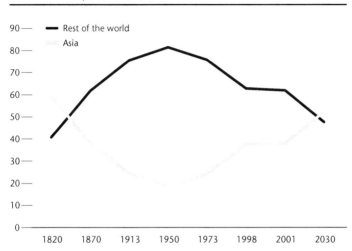

For 1820–2001 see World Population, GDP and Per Capita GDP, 1-2003 AD:
http://www.ggdc.net/maddison/Historical_Statistics/horizontal-file_03-2007.xls
For 2030 see World Development and Outlook 1820–2030: Evidence submitted to The House of
Lords: http://www.ggdc.net/maddison/articles/world_development_and_outlook_1820-
1930_evidence_submitted_to_the%20house_of_lords.pdf
Source: Angus Maddison

enterprises accounted for an astounding 60 per cent of merchandise trade (Table 5). Thus the world's most populous nation has, in quick time, mutated from almost complete autarchy to assume the characteristics of a small-to-medium-sized open economy like South Korea.

India's global integration pales in comparison, but it has come far by its own standards. By 2005, it was the world's sixteenth-largest trading nation in goods and the sixth-largest in services trade. Its share of world trade in goods and services was just under

Figure 16 **Japan, China and India's share of global GDP %**
1990, international $m

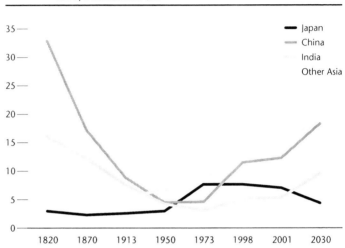

For 1820–2001 see World Population, GDP and Per Capita GDP, 1-2003 AD:
http://www.ggdc.net/maddison/Historical_Statistics/horizontal-file_03-2007.xls
For 2030 see World Development and Outlook 1820–2030: Evidence submitted to The House of
Lords: http://www.ggdc.net/maddison/articles/world_development_and_outlook_1820-
1930_evidence_submitted_to_the%20house_of_lords.pdf
Source: Angus Maddison

2 per cent, compared with over 8 per cent for China.[8] Trade and
FDI stock were 30 per cent and 6 per cent of GDP respectively –
way below China, but still registering fast growth from a very low
base. Annual FDI flows (about $6 billion) and overall FDI stock
(just over $30 billion) were under a tenth of Chinese levels (Table
5). Other South Asian countries have also seen global integration

---

8   I am grateful to Roderick Abbott for these estimates, calculated from the WTO's
     International Trade Statistics 2005, WTO, Geneva, 2006. All figures and rankings
     exclude intra-EU trade.

and economic progress, but this has been hampered by severe political instability and ethnic strife.

Finally, countries in South-East Asia are highly dependent on the world economy. Like China, FDI-driven exports are central to their growth models. South-East Asian trade levels are now lower than China's, which represents rapid Chinese trade growth and catch-up over the past decade. But they still dwarf Indian trade levels. The average trade-to-GDP ratio in South-East Asia is about 140 per cent. FDI inflows (at about $36 billion in 2005) are about half Chinese levels but way ahead of Indian levels (Table 5).

What does this tell us about the emerging international and Asian division of labour? Japan, South Korea, Taiwan, Hong Kong and Singapore have a comparative advantage in high-value goods and services. China has a clear-cut comparative advantage in labour-intensive manufacturing exports, and increasingly in labour-intensive agricultural exports.

Given its huge pool of cheap labour, India too should be a labour-intensive, FDI-driven exporting powerhouse in industrial goods, as well as a budding exporter of labour-intensive agricultural products. But severe labour-market restrictions strangulate industrial employment. Fewer than 10 million Indians are employed in the formal manufacturing sector, out of a total employable population of about 450 million. This compares with upwards of 150 million Chinese in manufacturing employment. Indian agriculture is hobbled by external and internal trade restrictions – much more so than in China. And the employment-generation effect from services exports is a drop in the ocean compared with what it could be in manufacturing. The much-hyped IT sector employs only 1 million relatively skilled and educated people.

South-East Asia in between stands to gain from deeper

Table 5 **Asian countries: economic and trade indicators, 2005**

Countries	GDP	GDP growth	Population	Per capita GDP	PPP GDP
	(US$ bn)	(%)	(mn)	(US$)	(US$ bn)
China	2,228.9	9.9	1,304.5	1,708.6	8572.7
Indonesia	287.2	5.6	220.6	1,302.2	847.4
Malaysia	130.1	5.3	25.3	5,134.4	274.8
Philippines	98.3	5.1	83.1	1,183.6	408.6
Singapore	116.8	6.4	4.4	26836.1	130.2
Thailand	176.6	4.5	64.2	2,749.4	549.3
Vietnam	52.4	8.4	83.0	631.7	254.0
ASEAN-6	861.4	5.9	480.6	1,792.3	2464.3
India	785.5	8.5	1,094.6	717.6	3815.5
Japan	4,505.9	2.7	128.0	35,214.5	3943.7
Korea	787.6	4.0	48.3	16,309.0	1056.1
Taipei	346.4	4.1	22.7	15,291.8	-
Hong Kong	177.7	7.3	6.9	25,593.6	214.5
TOTAL/AVE	9,693.4	–	3,085.6	3,141.5	20066.8
World	44,384.9	4.0	6,437.8	6,894.4	61006.6

* Whole of Taiwan.
Source: See the WTO Statistical Database for GDP, population, per capita GDP, merchandise exports, service exports, total merchandise trade, service trade; World Bank Key Development Data & Statistics for GDP growth; the UNCTAD FDI Statistics website for FDI inflows and FDI inward stock. World figures are collected from the World Bank Development Indicators database and Taipei GDP growth figures from the ADB Millennium Development Goals statistical tables.

integration into East Asian manufacturing supply chains, now including China. It is this 'Factory Asia' phenomenon (i.e. cross-border networks of 'fragmentation-based' trade and investment) which has driven phenomenal growth in trade between China, north-east and South-East Asia during the past decade. But to exploit these niches fully, the older ASEAN members must liberalise further, especially in services and agriculture, and strengthen domestic institutions in order to compensate for now-eroded

Merchandise exports	Service exports	Total merchandise trade	Services trade	Trade/ GDP	FDI Inflow	FDI inward stock / GDP
(US$ bn)	(US$ bn)	(US$ bn)	(US$ bn)	(%)	(US$ bn)	(%)
761.9	73.9	1,422.0	157.1	63.8	72.4	14.3
86.2	5.1	155.7	22.3	54.2	5.3	7.4
140.9	18.95	255.6	40.5	196.5	4.0	36.7
41.3	4.5	88.7	10.3	99.2	1.1	14.3
229.6	45.1	429.7	89.1	367.9	20.1	160.1
110.1	20.5	228.3	48.0	129.3	3.7	32.0
31.6	3.9	68.1	8.6	130.0	2.0	59.4
639.7	98.05	1,226.1	218.8	142.3	36.2	41.5
95.1	56.1	229.9	108.3	29.3	6.6	5.8
595.0	107.9	1,109.8	240.5	24.6	2.8	2.2
284.4	43.9	545.7	101.7	69.3	7.2	8.0
197.8	25.6	380.3	57.1	109.8	1.6*	12.1*
292.1	62.2	592.3	94.6	333.3	35.9	299.9
2,866.0	467.65	5,506.1	978.1	–	162.7	–
10,392.5	2,452.0	21,045.1	4,827.3	47.4	916.3	22.8

cheap-labour advantage. The newer, poorer ASEAN members should exploit their cheap-labour advantage, especially as relative incomes rise in China. India and the rest of South Asia remain very far from being integrated into East Asian supply chains.

Asia-driven globalisation demands massive adjustments. It is triggering mounting protectionist pressures and threatens an anti-globalisation backlash. Labour-abundant East and South Asia stand to gain most through fast, catch-up, trade and investment-driven growth, which feeds through to poverty reduction and improvement of life-chances for the majority of people. Developed and other developing countries will gain too through exploitation of their comparative advantages in capital, land and resource-intensive products. But they will be under increasing pressure in labour-intensive products. This could squeeze not just unskilled and low-skilled workers' real incomes, but also those of the middle classes. Thus the future holds out the prospect of greater prosperity overall, but perhaps with bigger inequality within and between nations. The political challenge is to keep borders open and extend market-based reforms, while containing inevitable protectionist pressures.

Asian trade-policy reforms

Chapter 3 discussed the global climate for trade policy pre- and post-Asian crisis. Broadly speaking, previous liberalisation of trade and FDI has not been reversed, but its forward momentum has slowed. How do East and South Asia fit into this global picture?

South-East Asia fits the pattern. With the exception of Singapore, government enthusiasm for further liberalisation and domestic structural reforms declined markedly during and after the Asian crisis. Overall, South-East Asia presents a varied picture: free-trade Singapore is at one extreme; other old ASEAN members have relatively liberal trade policies (with average tariffs under 10 per cent, correspondingly low non-tariff barriers (NTBs) and relatively open FDI regimes in manufacturing), but with large pockets of protection in agriculture and services; and the new ASEAN members are still highly protected (see Tables 6 and 7). Of the latter, Vietnam stands out as an exception: it has accelerated external liberalisation and internal reforms in the run-up to its WTO accession, and is now rapidly integrating into the global economy through FDI-driven exports.[9]

What about China? 'Reform' and 'Opening' started in 1978, but the whirlwind transformation of China's economy belongs more to the post-Tiananmen phase, especially since 1994. The unification and convertibility of the exchange rate, privatisation, the formal recognition of private property rights and a host of other market-based reforms have followed. Trade liberalisation whittled down the protective impact of border non-tariff barriers to about 5 per cent of imports on the eve of WTO accession in 2001; and the simple average tariff came down from 42 per cent in 1992 to 16.6 per cent in 2001, and then to about 10 per cent after WTO accession (Tables 6 and 7). This brings border barriers down to South-East Asian levels, and well below the developing-country average.

Thus China undertook enormous trade-and-FDI liberalisation, and with it sweeping industrial and agricultural restructuring, in the decade *before* WTO accession. Its accession to the WTO, after fourteen years of arduous negotiation, locked in these unilateral reforms and took them several steps further.[10] China's WTO commitments are very strong.[11] They exceed those of other

9 See Razeen Sally and Rahul Sen, 'Whither trade policies in southeast Asia? The wider Asian and global context', as well as individual country papers, all in *ASEAN Economic Bulletin*, 22(1), April 2005, Special Issue on 'Revisiting trade policies in Southeast Asia'.

10 Nicholas Lardy, *Integrating China into the Global Economy*, Brookings Institution, Washington, DC, 2002.

11 See *Report of the Working Party on the Accession of China*, the *Draft Protocol on the Accession of the People's Republic of China*, and attached Annexes with schedules of concessions on goods and services, all in WT/MIN(01)/3 at *www.wto.org* ; Elena Ianchovichina and Will Martin, 'Trade liberalisation in China's accession to the

developing countries by a wide margin. Indeed, they are almost as strong as developed countries' WTO commitments and are much stronger than those of other large developing countries such as India, Brazil, Egypt and Nigeria. They are also stronger than those of smaller, open economies in South-East Asia. These comparisons hold not only for tariff ceilings on goods (including agriculture), but also for border and behind-the-border non-tariff barriers in goods *and* services. For example: the average import-weighted GATT bound tariff is 6.8 per cent. Trading rights have been fully liberalised; nearly all quotas, licences, specific tendering arrangements and price controls have been removed; and there are strong disciplines on state trading enterprises, remaining subsidies and other non-tariff barriers. China has adopted WTO agreements on trade procedures, such as the TRIPS and TRIMS (Trade Related Investment Measures) agreements, in full and without transition periods. In services, the impact of WTO accession is, roughly, to cut protection by half. This is the most radical services-liberalisation programme ever seen. Finally, there are detailed commitments on transparency procedures to make sure trade-related laws and regulations are implemented, backed up by administrative and judicial-review procedures to which individuals and firms have recourse. This is nothing short of fundamental legal innovation in China.

Indian trade-policy reforms have not been as dramatic, but have still been considerable by Indian standards. In 1991, the

World Trade Organisation', World Bank Policy Research Working Paper 2623, June 2001, *www.worldbank.org*; Aaditya Mattoo, 'China's accession to the WTO: the services dimension,' *Journal of International Economic Law*, 6(2), 2003, pp. 299–339; Deepak Bhattasali, Li Shantong and Will Martin, *China's Accession to the World Trade Organisation, Policy Reform and Poverty Reduction*, World Bank, Washington, DC, 2004.

average unweighted tariff was 125 per cent, with peak tariffs on agricultural products going up to 300 per cent. The tariff structure was extremely complicated, and accompanied by extremely high non-tariff barriers. Inward investment was either banned or severely restricted. Exchange controls and the internal restrictions of the licence raj (almost) completed the picture.

Much has changed sixteen years on. Most border non-tariff barriers have been removed, as have internal licensing restrictions. Applied tariffs came down to an average of about 28 per cent by 2003/04, and farther down to about 16 per cent by 2005. The maximum tariff on manufactures was progressively lowered to 12.5 per cent by 2007. The intention is to bring average tariffs down to ASEAN levels (around 10 per cent) soon. Most restrictions on manufacturing FDI have been removed. In agriculture, however, tariffs and non-tariff barriers remain much higher (Table 6). And severe FDI and domestic regulatory restrictions keep out foreign competition in several big-ticket services sectors.[12]

Since the initial burst in 1991–93, Indian trade and other economic reforms have proceeded in a stop-go manner. They have not been reversed; but they have moved ahead more slowly and fitfully compared with South-East Asia (pre-Asian crisis) and China (pre- and post-Asian crisis). Democratic politics, including the complications of multi-party governing coalitions and the federal division of powers between the Union government and the states, has made faster, more decisive reforms elusive.

Japan, South Korea and Taiwan are relatively open economies after decades of gradual liberalisation, but all three have sent

---

12 *Trade Policy Review: India 2007*, WT/TPR/S/182, 18 April, WTO, Geneva, 2007, *www.wto.org/english/tratop_e/trp_e/s182-00_e.doc*; Aaditya Mattoo and Robert Stern (eds), *India and the WTO*, World Bank/OUP, Washington, DC, 2003.

Table 6 **Bound and applied MFN tariffs in selected countries**

	Binding coverage	Bound tariff rate (all goods)	Applied tariff rate (manufactures)	Applied tariff rate (agriculture)	Overall applied tariff
Japan	99.6	5.0	3.3	10.4	4.7
Korea	94.4	16.1	6.6	42.5	11.9
China	100	10.0	9.5	15.0	10.3
Hong Kong	45.7	0.0	0.0	0.0	0.0
Malaysia	83.7	14.5	8.1	2.1	7.3
Thailand	74.7	25.7	14.6	16.2	14.7
Indonesia	96.6	37.1	6.1	8.0	6.4
Philippines	66.8	25.6	6.9	11.8	7.5
Vietnam	–	–	12.9	18.1	13.7
Taiwan	100.0	6.1	5.5	16.3	6.9
Singapore	69.2	6.9	0.0	0.0	0.0
India	73.8	49.8	25.3	30.0	28.3
Pakistan	44.3	52.4	16.1	13.9	15.9
Bangladesh	15.8	163.8	19.2	21.7	19.5
Sri Lanka	37.8	29.8	9.6	15.4	10.2
South Africa	96.5	19.1	5.3	9.1	5.8
Brazil	100.0	31.4	11.0	10.4	10.9
Chile	100.0	25.1	5.9	6.0	5.9
Mexico	100.0	34.9	14.7	26.4	15.9
Australia	97.0	9.9	4.6	1.1	4.2
New Zealand	99.9	10.3	3.4	1.7	3.2

Note: The figures are simple unweighted averages of the tariff rates in per cent from 2003 and 2004.
Source: World Bank trade databases, http://siteresources.worldbank.org/INTRES/ Resources/469232–1107449512766/tar2005a.xls

mixed signals on market-based reforms recently. Japan and South Korea have been reluctant to liberalise trade and FDI further (though South Korea did partially open its financial sector as part of an IMF bailout package). Taiwan did liberalise substantially in the run-up to its WTO accession in 2001, though structural reforms have slowed down since.

Table 7 **Coverage ratio of non-tariff barriers in import trade***
(unweighted, %)

	1984–87	*1988–90*	*1991–93*	*1997–2000*
China	10.6	23.2	11.3	5.7
Indonesia	94.7	9.4	2.7	3.1
Korea	8.8	4.0	2.6	1.5
Malaysia	3.7	2.8	2.1	2.3
Philippines	44.9	n/a	n/a	1.8
Thailand	12.4	8.5	5.5	2.1

* Calculated as percentage of import value of HS6 tariff lines affected by NTBs
in total imports. NTBs include quantitative restrictions in the form of all types of
licences and import authorisation, quotas, import prohibitions, advanced import
deposits, foreign exchange restrictions, fixed customs valuations, and state trading
monopolies. Figures reported under a given sub-period relate to a single year within
that sub-period.
Sources: B. Hoekman, 'Economic development and the WTO after Doha', World
Bank Policy Research Working Paper no. 2851, Washington, DC, June 2002, Table
A-4; WTO, *Trade Policy Review* – Country Report (various). In Athukorala et al., 'Tariff
reform and the structure of protection in Thailand', Mimeo, 2 April 2004, p. 27

Unilateralism in Asia

The reader may wonder how Asia's trade-policy reforms and its
global economic integration relate to my stress on unilateral liberalisation and scepticism regarding trade negotiations. The bottom
line is this: first the north-east and South-East Asian tigers, and
then China and India, have done most of their trade-and-FDI
liberalisation unilaterally, not through bilateral, regional or multilateral negotiations.

Nowhere has unilateral liberalisation been stronger than in
East Asia, especially in the 1980s and 1990s (see Figure 17 for tariff
reductions in the region). In the 1980s, the old ASEAN countries
reduced import and inward-investment barriers simultaneously
in order to attract Japanese manufacturing multinational enterprises (which relied on imports of capital goods and components

for labour-intensive local processing and assembly of goods for export). This is how they inserted themselves into regional and global manufacturing supply chains, first in electronics and then spreading to other industries (e.g. sports footwear, televisions and radio receivers, office equipment, electrical machinery, power and machine tools, cameras and watches, and printing and publishing). In the 1990s, China also undertook unilateral and simultaneous trade and inward investment liberalisation, and thereby inserted itself as the cheap-labour, final-assembly stage in these expanding supply chains. This in turn triggered additional unilateral liberalisation by the South-East Asian countries. More openness to trade and FDI allowed the more advanced ASEAN countries to move up to higher-value production of parts and components in 'Factory Asia', while more labour-intensive production migrated to China, and more recently to Vietnam. To repeat: these measures were not fundamentally brought about by GATT/WTO, ASEAN Free Trade Area (AFTA) or other Free Trade Agreements (FTAs): they were unilateral responses to market conditions, resulting in market-led regional and global integration.[13]

China's external liberalisation now matters most, for it is the biggest the world has ever seen, with the biggest spillover effect in Asia. Most of this was done unilaterally, *before* WTO accession. China's WTO commitments, and its pragmatic, businesslike participation in the WTO since accession, are more the consequence than the cause of its sweeping unilateral reforms. Indeed, China is in many ways today what Britain was in the second half

---

13   Richard Baldwin, 'Multilateralising regionalism', op. cit.; Richard Baldwin, 'Implications of European experiences with regionalism for future economic integration in Asia', op. cit.; Athukorala, 'Product fragmentation and trade patterns in east Asia', op. cit.

Figure 17   **Tariffs in East-Asia, import-weighted**
              1980–2001

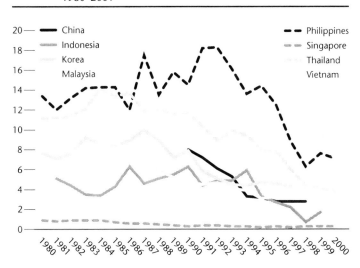

Source: Ando and Kimura (2005), which was drawn from Ando and Estevadeordal (2003) (Original data source: World Bank Indicators 2002 (CD-ROM)) and also used by Baldwin (2006)

of the nineteenth century: the unilateral engine of freer trade. True, China is far from being the top dog Britain was in the nineteenth century. But it is now the most powerful signal-transmitter in the Asian neighbourhood. China's opening not only spurred South-East Asian liberalisation before the Asian crisis; it probably helped to prevent liberalisation reversal after the Asian crisis. It has also encouraged East Asian countries to liberalise further at the margin since the Asian crisis – for fear of losing trade and FDI to China. Not least, China has probably had a knock-on effect on Indian opening to the world economy. India has recently accelerated its liberalisation of tariffs, and eased FDI restrictions in some services sectors. This has occurred outside trade negotiations, as was the case with previous Indian trade-and-investment liberalisation since 1991. Would this have happened, or happened as fast, if China had not concentrated minds? Probably not.

For other East and South Asian countries to take advantage of the opportunities offered by China's global integration, and overcome more-exposed weaknesses caused by protectionist policies and weak institutions, there has to be further liberalisation and regulatory reform. This is less likely to come about through the WTO, PTAs and regional institutions such as ASEAN and SAFTA, and more likely to result from unilateral measures by individual governments in response to internal and external conditions. That is the best prospect for East Asian countries to integrate themselves better into, and reap the benefits from, expanding regional and global supply chains. And that is the best prospect for South Asian countries to insert themselves into these supply chains.

That is not to say that China-induced unilateralism is a total solution. It is unlikely to induce further external liberalisation in the developed world, and least of all in the USA, EU and Japan. In the developing world, its results will inevitably be patchy and messy. For instance, unilateral liberalisation in East Asia, while strong in fragmentation-based manufacturing products that feature in global supply chains, has been weaker in other areas of manufacturing, very uneven in services and especially weak in agriculture. More generally, unilateral measures do not lock in liberalisation against future backtracking. Above all, they do not provide fair, stable and predictable rules for international commerce. On its own, therefore, unilateral liberalisation cannot slay protectionist dragons and solve international commercial conflicts. That leaves room for the WTO and PTAs, but these are at best *second* instances of trade policy. The WTO in particular can be a helpful auxiliary, less in driving a future liberalisation agenda and more in providing a set of enforceable non-discriminatory rules for international commerce, not least to assist developing-country governments in undertaking market-based reforms. But it is important to get priorities right and follow the process bottom-up and not top-down.

China and the unilateral progress to freer trade: post-Doha priorities

As I have argued, trade policy across Asia looks rather unbalanced. It rests on a shaky PTA leg. Its other WTO leg has gone to sleep; its regional-cooperation arm is limp; and, above all, core abdominal strength through unilateral reforms has weakened after the Asian crisis. China is the conspicuous exception. With the collapse of the Doha Round, the Gadarene rush to do more dirty PTAs, and the consequent fraying of the multilateral trading system, three new priorities are called for.

Asia's role

First, China, India, Japan, South Korea, Hong Kong and the ASEAN countries should be active in plurilateral 'coalitions of the willing' to restore the WTO's fortunes, albeit in a sober, realistic manner. This will require US leadership and the cooperation of other major powers. China's helping hand will be indispensable. Once the dust of the Doha Round settles, it is vital that China moves to the WTO foreground and plays an active co-leadership role.

Second, there should be much more caution with PTAs. Existing PTAs should be cleaned up, and new initiatives launched only with a credible economic strategy. Again, China's lead will be important. It needs to signal its intention to go for strong and clean FTAs, and avoid weak and dirty FTAs. Others will take the hint.

These two points recapitulate what I have said in the previous two chapters. But there is a *third* priority, more important than the other two. It is vital that the Chinese engine of unilateral liberalisation does not stall: further global trade-and-FDI liberalisation, and related domestic structural reforms, depend on it. Short of a global crisis to concentrate minds, there is no replacement engine for trade-related reforms in Asia and elsewhere.

The role of Europe and the USA

But this Chinese engine is not pre-programmed. The Beijing leadership is less visionary and more cautious, and domestic protectionist lobbies are more vocal, than was the case at the beginning of the decade. Reforms are now in more politically sensitive territory as they bite deeper into domestic regulation and institutions. The momentum for reform continues, but with greater political opposition and at a slower pace. Consequently, the Beijing leadership is likely to go much farther with liberalisation and structural reforms only if it faces a reasonably clement external macroeconomic and trade environment. This is probably necessary to overcome domestic opposition to change, especially within the Communist Party and the public sector. Tub-thumping protectionism and belligerence by the USA and EU about issues such as the Chinese exchange rate and current-account surplus, and imports of garments and other labour-intensive exports, as well as on security-related issues, will invite a Chinese backlash and make its leadership more defensive. That is likely to result in a slowdown in reform.

Thus it behoves the USA in the first instance, and then the EU, to strengthen 'constructive engagement' with China across a broad range of economic and foreign-policy issues, while containing foreign-policy hawks and protectionist forces at home. This will, in turn, encourage Beijing to strengthen its key bilateral relationships and its participation in international institutions, contain occasionally aggressive nationalistic tendencies (especially directed at Taiwan and Japan), and, not least, keep up the momentum of economic reforms.[14] Such an alignment will encourage others, such as India, the ASEAN countries, Japan and South Korea, to act in the same vein. All this is more a matter of unilateral example-setting and bilateral cooperation than of trade negotiations.

Conclusion

China is driving Asia's transformation of the world economy but is doing so largely outside trade negotiations. The challenge in China, India and elsewhere in the developing world is to go farther with economic reforms: more trade-and-investment liberalisation; much more internal liberalisation to integrate

---

14 This is the coda to Robert Zoellick's much-publicised speech on US–China relations, 'Whither China: from membership to responsibility?' Remarks to the National Committee on US–China Relations, New York City, 21 September 2005, *www.state.gov/s/d/rem/53682.htm*. It is also the underlying logic of the US–China Strategic Economic Dialogue, established in late 2006 following the initiative of US Treasury Secretary Hank Paulson.

the domestic market; and more second-generation institutional reforms to restructure the state so that it supports, not hinders, a complex, globally integrated market economy. The external corollary of economic-policy reforms at home is to anchor constructive engagement abroad and make it permanent, not hostage to the vagaries of a few personalities and stray events.

On that canvas of global politics and economics, the trade-policy challenges of the future will be less amenable to the top-down bureaucratic solutions of the past. Trade-policy reforms will be increasingly of the second-generation variety. They will have to tackle non-border regulatory barriers that impede trade, foreign investment and the cross-border movement of workers. These barriers lie deep in domestic policies and institutions. They concern property rights and the legal system, public administration, state-owned enterprises, capital markets, labour markets, services regulation, intellectual property, competition and investment rules, customs administration, public procurement, product standards, corporate law and bankruptcy procedures, and other issues besides. Related reforms are technically complicated, locally specific, administratively demanding and politically very sensitive. They are bundled up with domestic politics and economics; initiating and implementing them is overwhelmingly a domestic affair; and the scope for productive international negotiations and solutions is restricted. And it is precisely in all these areas that China and India still do very badly – as the World Bank's business-climate and governance indicators show (see Tables 8 and 9 on red-tape barriers to business, trade and governance in Asian countries, and Table 10 on governance indicators in Asian countries).

To sum up: freer trade in the early 21st century and modern

Table 8 **World ranking in ease of doing business, 2007**

	Ease of doing business	Starting a business	Dealing with licences	Employing workers	Registering property	Getting credit	Protecting investors	Paying taxes	Trading across borders	Enforcing contracts	Closing a business
Singapore	1	9	5	1	13	7	2	2	1	4	2
Hong Kong	4	13	60	23	58	2	3	3	3	1	15
Japan	12	44	32	17	48	13	12	105	18	21	1
Thailand	15	36	12	49	20	36	33	89	50	26	44
Malaysia	24	74	105	43	67	3	4	56	21	63	54
Korea	30	110	22	131	68	36	64	106	13	10	11
Taiwan	50	103	128	148	24	48	64	91	29	92	13
Pakistan	76	59	93	132	88	68	19	146	94	154	51
China	83	135	175	86	29	84	83	168	42	20	57
Vietnam	91	97	63	84	38	48	165	128	63	40	121
Sri Lanka	101	29	160	111	134	97	64	158	60	133	39
Bangladesh	107	92	116	129	171	48	15	81	112	175	102
Philippines	107	92	116	129	171	48	15	81	112	175	102
India	120	111	134	85	112	36	33	165	79	177	137
Indonesia	123	168	99	153	121	68	51	110	41	141	136

Note: The numbers correspond to each country's aggregate ranking on the ease of doing business and on each of the ten topics that comprise the overall ranking.

Source: World Bank Doing Business database

Table 9 **Indicators for trading across borders, 2007**

	Ease of trading across borders (world ranking)	Documents for export (number)	Time for export (days)	Cost to export (US$ per container)	Documents for import (number)	Time for import (days)	Cost to import (US$ per container)
Singapore	1	4	5	416	4	3	367
Hong Kong	3	4	6	525	4	5	525
Korea	13	4	11	745	6	10	745
Japan	18	4	10	989	5	11	1,047
Malaysia	21	7	18	432	7	14	385
Taiwan	29	7	13	747	7	12	747
Indonesia	41	5	21	667	6	27	623
China	42	7	21	390	6	24	430
Thailand	50	7	17	615	9	14	786
Philippines	57	8	17	800	8	18	800
Sri Lanka	60	8	21	810	6	21	844
Vietnam	63	6	24	669	8	23	881
India	79	8	18	820	9	21	910
Pakistan	94	9	24	515	8	19	1,336
Bangladesh	112	7	28	844	9	32	1,148

Note: The costs and procedures involved in importing and exporting a standardised shipment of goods are detailed under this topic. Every official procedure involved is recorded – starting from the final contractual agreement between the two parties, and ending with the delivery of the goods.

Source: World Bank Doing Business database

Table 10 **Percentile world rank of governance indicators for Asian countries, 2006**

	Voice and accountability	Political stability/ no violence	Government effectiveness	Regulatory quality	Rule of law	Control of corruption
Singapore	46.6	94.7	99.5	99.5	95.2	98.1
Hong Kong	64.9	88.9	93.8	100.0	90.5	92.7
Japan	75.5	85.1	88.2	87.3	90.0	90.3
Malaysia	38.0	58.7	80.6	69.8	65.7	68.0
Taiwan	72.1	63.5	83.9	78.5	74.8	70.4
Korea	70.7	60.1	82.9	70.7	72.9	64.6
India	58.2	22.1	54.0	48.3	57.1	52.9
Thailand	32.2	16.3	64.9	62.4	55.2	50.5
China	4.8	33.2	55.5	46.3	45.2	37.9
Vietnam	8.2	59.6	41.7	31.2	44.8	29.1
Indonesia	41.3	14.9	40.8	43.4	23.3	23.3
Sri Lanka	36.1	8.2	42.2	50.2	54.3	48.5
Philippines	44.2	11.1	55.0	52.2	41.9	27.2
Bangladesh	30.8	8.7	23.7	20.0	22.9	4.9
Pakistan	12.5	4.8	34.1	38.5	24.3	18.0

Note: Percentile rank indicates the percentage of countries worldwide that rate below the country (subject to margin of error). Higher values indicate better governance ratings. Percentile ranks have been adjusted to account for changes over time in the set of countries covered by the governance indicators.
Source: World Bank governance indicators

globalisation more generally are happening more 'from below' than 'from above'. Their engine, now to be found in Asia, particularly in China, is bottom-up liberalisation and regulatory reform that spreads through competitive emulation, like ripples and waves across seas and oceans. This process is not driven by international institutions. As the German economist Wilhelm Röpke noted: 'internationalism, like charity, begins at home'; it emerges 'from within and beneath'; like a house, it cannot be built 'starting with the roof'; and 'more important than international institutions and legal constructions are the moral-political forces behind the market that are only really effective within nations'.[15]

---

15   Wilhelm Röpke, *International Order and Economic Integration*, Reidel, Dordrecht, 1959, pp. 9–20.

7 CONCLUSION: THE FUTURE OF FREE TRADE

Beginning with David Hume and Adam Smith, the emphasis on free trade has been not just one of the postulates, but the very heart or essence, of economic liberalism.

JAN TUMLIR

In political activity, then, men sail a boundless and bottomless sea; there is neither harbour for shelter nor floor for anchorage, neither starting point nor appointed destination. The enterprise is to keep afloat on an even keel; the sea is both friend and enemy; and the seamanship consists in using resources of a traditional manner of behaviour to make a friend of every hostile occasion.

MICHAEL OAKESHOTT

This book has taken stock of trade policy in the early 21st century. It began with an intellectual history of free trade versus protection; then surveyed the political economy of trade-policy reform, especially in developing countries; then moved to the WTO, PTAs, unilateral liberalisation and the rise of Asia. Now, in closing, I shift from the present to the future of trade policy. What are the real-world prospects for free (or freer) trade in the years and decades ahead? How will it fare against existing and emerging protectionist threats? And how can one best make the case for free trade in the future?

Optimists will look forward to further advances for free trade in globalisation's wake. But others will be more pessimistic, or at least sound a cautionary note. Protectionism, they would say, lurks everywhere. It is safe to say that protectionism will still be around in mid-century, and the battle between it and free trade will continue to rage. That is one clear lesson from economic history and the history of ideas.

The quotes above hint at the balance I seek. They juxtapose the classical-liberal free-trade ideals of Jan Tumlir with the pragmatism expressed in one of Michael Oakeshott's most quoted passages. Free trade is a desirable goal, and progress in that direction, however gradual and piecemeal, should be integral to modern globalisation. But politics is a practical, messy affair. To borrow Oakeshott's seafaring metaphor, the ship of state has trouble enough to stay afloat on an even keel in turbulent seas. Sensible political economy has to factor this in. That is what I have tried to do in the previous chapters. The question now is how it applies to the future of free trade.

The first sections of this chapter review free trade today, in theory and in practice. The following sections look ahead. What are the emerging facts on the ground in terms of global political and economic trends? And what of the case for free trade in the future?

Taking stock: the case for free trade, past and present

Chapter 2 summarised the main political and economic arguments in favour of free trade. To recapitulate: meta-economic arguments for free trade date back at least two millennia. An intellectual tradition from early Christian thought to Richard Cobden, Woodrow Wilson and Cordell Hull holds that open and

flourishing international commerce brings about better understanding between peoples and buttresses peaceful, ever-closer
international relations.

The *economic* case for free trade emerged one and a half
millennia later. Adam Smith's genius was to draw on pre-existing
traditions of moral philosophy and economics to lay out a system
of interrelating economic phenomena animated by laissez-faire, or
what he called 'natural liberty'. This he extended to international
trade.

Smith's system has been refined down the past two centuries.
An international division of labour according to comparative
advantage allocates resources more efficiently, resulting in the
greater wealth of nations. It integrates hitherto separated national
economies into a worldwide *cooperative* system that caters for
reciprocal wants. There are all-round material gains, for rich and
poor countries alike.

These are the short-term (or static) gains from trade. That
is but the necessary preface for capital accumulation, economies of scale and other long-run (or dynamic) gains, such as
the transfer of technology and skills, and the competitive spur
that comes from exposure to world-class standards of practice.
This feeds into productivity gains, increases in real incomes and
economic growth. Indeed, it is the dynamic gains from trade
which Smith and his contemporary David Hume emphasised.
They strongly linked free trade (broadly defined to include
cross-border flows of capital and people) to domestic institutions and growth, all on the canvas of the long-run progress of
commercial society.

Adam Smith fortified his presumption in favour of free trade
with an explicit political argument. Protectionism is driven by 'the

clamorous importunity of partial interests' who capture government and prevent it from having 'an extensive view of the general good'. Free trade, in contrast, tilts the balance away from rent-seeking producer interests and towards the mass of consumers. It is part of a wider constitutional package to keep government limited, transparent and clean, enabling it to concentrate better on the public good.

As important to Smith and Hume was the *moral* case for free trade, centred on individual freedom. Individual choice is the engine of free trade, and of progressive commercial society more generally. It sparks what Hume called a 'spirit of industry'; it results in much better life-chances, not just for the select few but for individuals in the broad mass of society who are able to lead more varied and interesting lives.

To sum up: free trade is of course associated with standard economic efficiency arguments. But the classical-liberal case for free trade is more rounded, taking in the moral imperative of individual freedom and linking it to prosperity. Finally, free trade contributes to, though it does not guarantee, peaceful international relations. Freedom, prosperity, security: this trinity lies at the heart of the case for free trade.

Taking stock: free trade in practice

Chapter 3 argued that the historical record shows that countries that are more open to the world economy perform better than those that are less open or remain closed. This of course runs counter to the assertions of sceptics of liberalisation and globalisation.

External trade has been a 'handmaiden' of growth since

classical antiquity.[1] Trade across frontiers promoted 'Smithian' growth (real-income gains from the integration of geographically separated markets) in ancient Greece and Rome, during the Sung period in China, at the time of the Mauryas in India and the Abbasids in the Middle East, and in the Europe of the Middle Ages. Smithian growth continues apace in developed and developing countries. Since the Industrial Revolution it has been supplemented by the 'Promethean' growth powered by successive technological revolutions.[2]

The evidence of the past two centuries, roughly since the post-Napoleonic settlement, supports the proposition that economies grow faster and get richer the more open they become. One of Lord Bauer's chief insights was that economic advancement in the developing world has occurred in countries and regions that have had the most contact with the outside world, and particularly with the advanced centres of the world economy in the West. Indeed, no country on earth has seen a sustained rise in living standards without being open to the world.[3]

The more detailed evidence post-1945 points in the same direction. The gradual liberalisation of trade and capital flows in the Organisation for Economic Cooperation and Development (OECD) spurred Western European reconstruction, recovery and catch-up growth. The outward orientation of Japan and other East

---

1   The concept of international trade as a handmaiden of growth comes from Irving Kravis. See his 'Trade as a handmaiden of growth: similarities between the nineteenth and twentieth centuries', *Economic Journal*, LXXX, 1970, pp. 850–72.

2   Deepak Lal, *Unintended Consequences: The Impact of Factor Endowments, Culture and Politics on Long-Run Economic Performance*, MIT Press, Cambridge, MA, 1998.

3   Peter Bauer, 'Western guilt and Third World poverty', in *From Subsistence to Exchange and Other Essays*, op. cit., pp. 57–9.

Asian countries played an important role in their catch-up growth. The massive liberalisation of foreign trade and inward investment in China, in tandem with internal liberalisation, has contributed to spectacular and sustained growth since the 1980s. Similar forces have been at work in India since the 1990s. Hence liberalisation of trade and FDI is central to Asia's unfolding transformation of the global economy. Strong liberalisers elsewhere have also reaped growth and welfare gains, notably eastern European countries, Chile, Australia and New Zealand.

Such is the good news for the bulk of the world's population that live in the OECD plus about twenty-five 'new-globalising' developing countries. The bad news is that this leaves about 1.5 billion people in over fifty less-globalised, worse-performing countries. These are low-income and least-developed countries that have liberalised less, though they suffer too from other intractable problems such as poor climate and geography, rampant disease, ethnic conflict, civil war and chronically corrupt, predatory governments.

External liberalisation, it must be emphasised, is not a panacea. Questions of how it is sequenced with other economic and political reforms, and whether it should proceed quickly or slowly, will find different answers in different countries at different times. Furthermore, trade liberalisation on its own may not deliver much. But *in interaction with* market-friendly domestic policies and institutions there are abundant, long-term gains to be had. External opening creates the spontaneous stimulus for institutional upgrading to better exploit trade and investment opportunities, e.g. through better currency and banking practices, and the development of ports and inland communications. Better enforcement of property rights and contracts, combined with cleaner and more efficient public administration, together with simpler and more transparent regulations for doing business, maximise the gains for importers, exporters and domestic and foreign investors. In these conditions the benefits of more investment in infrastructure can also be obtained. Openness, to repeat, is a *handmaiden* of growth, not a quick fix.

What of the policy framework to support a freer trading system? This was the subject of Chapters 4–6.

A workable WTO, focused on market access and supporting non-discriminatory rules, is important. But the WTO has not delivered, especially in the Doha Round. It is going to be very difficult to put the WTO on the right track. To do so, more modesty and realism is in order. The WTO is unlikely to deliver further substantial multilateral liberalisation. The best that can be hoped for is modest, incremental multilateral liberalisation where feasible. More important will be a stronger focus on safeguarding and improving vital multilateral trade rules.

PTAs are no substitute for a workable WTO. In certain conditions they can reinforce market reforms, but only if they are strong, comprehensive, WTO-plus, competition-enhancing agreements. Nearly all PTAs, though, are weak, trade-light and full of discriminatory provisions that potentially restrict trade – they are more fluffy foreign policy than commercially sensible arrangements. That is the emerging reality in Asia-Pacific, reflecting what has happened already in other developing-country regions. While today's PTAs do not presage a breakdown in the world trading system, their rampant discrimination is creating worrying political and economic complications.

That leaves the unilateral method as the driving force of external liberalisation in the developing world. Trade negotiations and agreements have their place, but unilateral liberalisation comes first. Now its engine is China. That, more than trade negotiations, is and will be the spur to further trade and FDI liberalisation elsewhere in Asia and beyond. It is vital that China continues with its trade and related domestic reforms. That depends on a host of internal and external political and economic conditions.

Looking ahead: world political-economic trends

As argued in Chapter 6, the new Asian Drama, particularly the opening of first China and then India, is a defining feature of early 21st-century globalisation. Developing Asia's transformation of the world economy, still in its early stages, promises to be as momentous as the entry of the USA, Germany and Japan into the world economy in the last third of the nineteenth century. It could even herald the biggest global economic transformation since the Industrial Revolution. These effects will unfold over the course of the next few decades. What are the implications?

Emerging trends show that the classical argument for free trade is as relevant as ever. Trade and related economic reforms enable China, India and other Asian countries to better exploit their comparative advantages in a more specialised international division of labour. Market-based reforms also provide the stimulus for inward investment, the transfer of technology and skills, and a more competitive, entrepreneurial business environment. These replenishing gains boost growth, which in turn leads to poverty reduction.

The rest of the world gains too. Consumers elsewhere can buy cheaper and more varied products. Developed-country firms cater to expanding Chinese and Indian demand for capital-intensive and skill-intensive inputs to local production, as well as for finished goods and services. By 'offshoring' low-value manufacturing and services activities, these firms can scale up, improve productivity and generate better-skilled, higher-paying jobs at home. Exporters in resource-abundant developed and developing countries are also discovering large new markets for commodities – witness China's voracious appetite for oil, gas, minerals, metals and agricultural commodities.

That said, these all-round comparative-advantage-based gains mask tensions and potential conflict. The effective doubling-to-quadrupling of the world's workforce since 1980 – very much the result of China's and India's insertion into the world economy – has shifted the relationship between global capital and labour. Labour-intensive exports from Asia are displacing cheap-labour activities while increasing returns to capital-intensive and knowledge-intensive activities in the West. As more tasks are 'unbundled' and offshored to developing countries, there is more pressure on mid-skilled activities performed by middle-class workers in the West. The net result is widening inequality, possibly now extending to middle-class incomes. The magnitude of these effects is still unclear, and perhaps prone to exaggeration. But the potential for them to bite deeper is evident, especially with more intensive North–South trade.[4]

Many developing countries without abundant natural resources also face a stiffer competitive challenge. This applies in particular to countries with labour-intensive manufacturing

---

[4]   See Martin Wolf's recent columns on the issue in the *Financial Times*: 'A divided world of economic success and political turmoil', 30 January 2007; 'A new gilded age', 25 April 2006; 'Confronting seismic economic shifts', 31 January 2006. Also see 'The new titans', *The Economist* Survey of the World Economy, 14 September 2006.

activities squeezed by Chinese competition and caught in a 'middle-income trap'.[5]

The danger is that wider inequality and a middle-class squeeze in the West, combined with the squeeze on developing countries caught in a middle-income trap, will undermine support for globalisation and lead to a protectionist backlash. This will be directed at China in the first instance, but also at India. This threatens to slow down globalisation and diminish its benefits – not just for developing countries with huge numbers of poor people, but also for the vast middle classes in the developed world.

What is to be done? Luddite protectionism, either in the West or in the developing world, is not the answer. It will benefit a minority of cosseted, politically well-connected producers and other rent-seekers at the expense of everyone else.

A seemingly more reasonable alternative is what could be labelled 'globalisation and social democracy'. This world-view is increasingly popular in policy-wonk circles in Europe and North America. It holds that borders must be kept open so that globalisation can deliver its benefits. But, within the border, governments should have an expansive, interventionist, redistributive role. This entails making taxation more progressive, supporting social-safety nets, targeting assistance at workers who lose their jobs as a result of imports, and providing infrastructure and public services such as healthcare, education and training. Active, enabling government is needed to 'compensate losers', shore up domestic support for globalisation and adapt economies to global competition.[6]

---

5   Alan Beattie, 'Avoiding the crush', *Financial Times*, 14 June 2007.
6   See Lawrence Summers's columns in the *Financial Times*: 'Harnessing market

In essence, globalisation combined with social democracy is an update of the post-1945 Bretton Woods compromise (otherwise known as 'Smith abroad and Keynes at home', or more clumsily as 'the compromise of embedded liberalism'). It also dovetails with the post-war theory of commercial policy, which holds that free trade abroad is compatible with government intervention to remedy domestic market failures (as outlined in Chapter 2).

The first part of the equation is correct: borders must be kept open so that globalisation can continue apace. And yes, this does require domestic political management to prevent a protectionist backlash. But the second, 'social-democratic' part of the equation is, in my view, incorrect. Governments do have a role in financing basic social-safety nets, education, healthcare and infrastructure. But this does not necessitate open-ended intervention. There is, after all, a long record of 'government failure' in these areas, in the West as well as in the rest of the world. Indeed, government failure is as prevalent at home as it is when governments interfere with international commerce. Overactive government rigidifies domestic labour markets and other aspects of economic activity – at a time when more, not less, flexibility is required so that national economies can adapt effectively to keener global competition.

Hence classical liberals would make a strong case for *limited* government at home as well as abroad, and for free trade (or laissez-faire) at home as well as abroad. Limited government – not to be confused with minimal government or a 'nightwatchman state'[7]

forces to share prosperity', 24 June 2007; 'Lack of fear gives cause for concern', 26 December 2006; 'The global middle class cries out for reassurance', 29 October 2006.

7   The perpetual caricature of classical liberalism is that it supports a nightwatchman state, a 'harmony-of-interests' doctrine and anarcho-capitalist laissez-faire.

– would eschew higher levels of taxation and complicated labour-market interventions. It would encourage, not discourage, competition among private-sector providers of infrastructure, health, education and training services. This should include opening up these sectors to international competition. Such measures would run with, not against, the grain of globalisation, which is blurring the divide between international and domestic activities by making swathes of the latter more tradeable. That includes public services traditionally run along command-economy lines.

My view is that a classical-liberal frame of limited government and free trade is better suited to adapting national economies to globalisation than the schizophrenia of globalisation combined with social democracy. In addition to underestimating government failure, the latter has different and contradictory sets of tools for the international and domestic spheres, premised on an increasingly untenable divide between what is 'international' and what is 'domestic'. Classical liberalism, in contrast, has complementary, market-based sets of tools for international and domestic policies, and makes no artificial distinction between the two spheres.

Other emerging global challenges

In addition to the new Asian Drama, there are other emerging global trends that are likely to move centre-stage in the years and decades to come. I will highlight several below.

First, the freedom of people to move in search of work was

That is not true. Hume, Smith, John Stuart Mill, Alfred Marshall, F. A. Hayek and others in the tradition never held these views. See Razeen Sally, *Classical Liberalism and International Economic Order*, op. cit., ch. 2.

part of nineteenth-century free trade in practice. This was reversed in the twentieth century. As did freeing up the international exchange of goods and services and capital mobility, loosening pervasive restrictions on cross-border labour movement promises large gains for developing and developed countries. It helps to plug labour shortages in rich countries with ageing and shrinking populations, and with relatively affluent people unwilling to do low-paid menial work. It provides an outlet for people in poor countries in search of a better life. In turn they remit large sums of money to families back home. If the incentives are right, many will go back to their homelands with capital, skills and contacts with world markets. Generally, hard-working migrants and temporary foreign workers inject energy and vitality into often complacent, decadent and vegetative societies.[8]

Still, a note of political and social realism is in order. Opening borders to people is much more sensitive than opening borders to trade and capital flows. International trade takes place 'in the company of strangers'; FDI is closer to home; but having foreigners as one's co-workers and neighbours is really up close.[9] There are legitimate concerns about assimilating people from very different cultures into liberal societies while preserving the rule of law and social stability. And there are understandable anxieties about an excessive 'multiculturalism' that tolerates foreign religious and other extremists who propagate intolerance and violence.

None of these concerns should detract from the basic case

---

8   Philippe Legrain, *Immigrants: Your Country Needs Them*, Little, Brown, London, 2006.

9   Paul Seabright, *The Company of Strangers*, Princeton University Press, Princeton, NJ, 2004.

for more open borders and the freer movement of people. But they do argue in favour of a cautious, gradual and controlled process – a long-term project akin to the half-century it took to liberalise tariffs under the GATT. This demands political patience and resourcefulness. Nevertheless, it should be at the heart of a 21st-century free-trade agenda.

Second, inter-developing-country trade – already 40 per cent of their overall trade – is throttled by the high barriers developing countries erect against each other. Significant developing-country liberalisation would not only improve their own productivity; it would also allow low-income and least-developed countries to better exploit their comparative advantage by exporting to middle-income developing countries, as well as to the fast-growing markets of China and India. It is incumbent on major regional powers, notably China, India, Brazil and South Africa, to unilaterally open their markets. That, more than the WTO and PTAs, would enable often blighted neighbouring countries to share in their growth and prosperity. It would also contribute to regional peace and stability.

Third, many developing countries are mired in wretched poverty, disease, crime and murderous internal strife. States are failing miserably or have collapsed. This affects much of Africa, but it is not restricted to Africa. Paul Collier estimates that close to 1 billion people – the 'bottom billion' – live in almost sixty such states.[10] The old solutions of aid and policy driven by international organisations have not worked. Grandiose blueprints for significantly more aid are highly unlikely to work. Nor is seemingly more modest World Bank thinking that better-performing states should

---

10   Paul Collier, *The Bottom Billion*, Oxford University Press, Oxford, 2007.

be rewarded with more and better-targeted aid. All such ideas are suffused with misguided top-down planning, political naivety and the self-serving interests of those in the aid business. But that still leaves failed and failing states with venal and thuggish ruling elites, and without the history and institutions to sustain market-based reforms 'from below'. The dilemma is real; problems may get worse; and they will spill over to luckier parts of the world in the form of refugees, illegal migrants and terrorism.

Paul Collier and others place some faith in targeted, 'smart' aid, not least to build or reconstruct the institutions necessary to support a market economy. They also advocate full (i.e. unrestricted) access to developed-country export markets. Optimists may concede a role for better-targeted aid on a case-by-case basis, with built-in market and transparency mechanisms (such as open auctions). And, yes, the West and advanced developing countries could help by removing all tariff and non-tariff barriers (including ROO restrictions and anti-dumping duties) to exports from 'bottom-billion' countries.

Nevertheless, it beggars belief that well-intentioned, better-designed aid will work on a big scale – once it runs into the irredeemably corrupt politics of the aid business. Furthermore, lack of access to Western markets is far from being the core problem facing bottom-billion countries: most already have generous preferential access to OECD countries. The EU's 'Everything but Arms' scheme, for example, gives least-developed countries almost unrestricted market access. Also, preferences are a curse, especially in the long term, but often in the short term as well. They cause trade diversion from other developing countries that continue to face higher trade barriers, shield least-developed and low-income countries from global competition, and encourage them to rely on external favours rather than adapt to market forces.

The bald reality is that the travails of bottom-billion countries have much more to do with internal failure than external market access. At best, externally driven solutions are bound to have limited beneficial effects. Hopefully, some countries will drag themselves to the path of growth and prosperity through enlightened political leadership, better governance, freer internal markets and comprehensive opening to the global economy. This they can do by emulating the 'new globalisers' in the developing world. But, as far as the bulk of bottom-billion countries are concerned, I remain pessimistic. This problem will be with us for generations to come.

Fourth, the 'low politics' of trade and related economic policies cannot be divorced from the 'high politics' of international security (or the lack of it). There are new global security flashpoints post-cold-war and post-September 11th: Islamic fundamentalism and the international terror networks fanning out from the oil-rich Middle East; military rivalry between established and rising powers, especially between the USA and China; and the scramble for energy resources, also involving competition among the powers. All threaten the free movement of people, goods and services across the world. It is all too tempting to use 'national security' as a cloak for protectionism. This has to be contained, and a sensible balance found between legitimate security goals and unfettered international commerce.

Fifth, investment nationalism is on the rise, and it is often twinned with energy nationalism. State-owned or state-linked energy companies from China, India and Russia are aggressively chasing markets and securing supplies abroad, aided and abetted by home-government industrial policy. There are more examples of OECD and developing-country governments discriminating against foreign investors in order to protect 'national champions'.

FDI is critically important to developed countries and newly globalising developing countries. There are now emerging multinationals from China, India and other developing countries. Hence there is an overriding general interest to prevent investment nationalism from getting out of hand, and to have simple, transparent and predictable rules to guarantee the freedom to invest abroad.

Sixth, the clamour to combat global warming risks becoming the new Trojan horse for protectionism. There may be a case for taking precautionary measures to deal with the threats posed by climate change, and these measures will require action at regional and global levels. But the climate-change debate is already full of hot air. The atmosphere is befogged with puffy ideas to subsidise this or that initiative and tax this or that 'environmental bad'. Climate change has rapidly become a lightning-rod issue for ad hoc, bureaucratic, costly interventions; and it could easily spill over into protection against imports. There is a wrong way to link trade policy to climate change. The right way is to take economically efficient precautionary measures (such as a simple carbon tax) while keeping borders open to international commerce.

Seventh, 'standards protectionism' is an established feature of trade policy. Onerous technical, food-safety, intellectual-property, labour and environmental standards are aimed at restricting mainly labour-intensive exports from developing countries. The pressure for greater 'standards harmonisation' can only increase; and with it comes what Jagdish Bhagwati calls 'regulatory intrusionism' that undermines developing countries' cost advantages.[11]

Product and other standards directly imposed by governments are not the only threat, however. The last decade has seen the rise of voluntarily agreed global standards on all manner of commercial activities, usually in the name of 'corporate social responsibility' and involving the cooperation of governments, multinational firms, NGOs and international organisations. So far the bulk of these standards have been of the 'soft' variety, without the sanction of national or international law. But there is pressure to make them 'harder' and more coercive, with government backing and legal sanction. This would widen the range of regulatory intrusion and back-door protectionism aimed at developing countries. Huge multinational firms may manage comfortably in this kind of world, but it threatens to restrict profitable commercial opportunities for smaller firms employing mostly poor workers. They are less able to bear the costs involved: that is the real danger of direct and indirect standards protectionism.[12]

Protectionist viruses need carriers. Organised rent-seeking interests that benefit directly from protectionism are long-standing carriers. Business groups and unionised labour in cahoots with politicians and bureaucrats are familiar culprits. But they would not be effective without powerful ideological opposition to free trade. The latter has changed form since the collapse of communism and the end of the cold war. The *sentimental*, post-communist and postmodern opposition to globalisation, and markets generally, is now led by a congeries of NGOs.

---

11   Bhagwati, op. cit., pp. 52–7.
12   David Henderson, *Misguided Virtue: False Notions of Corporate Social Responsibility*, Institute of Economic Affairs, London, 2004.

Globalisation, then, faces the opposition of an alliance, witting or not, between old-style rent-seeking interests and new-style ideological forces. One is reminded of John Stuart Mill's reference to 'the numerous sentimental enemies of political economy, and its still more numerous interested enemies in sentimental guise'.[13] Militant anti-globalisation activists are bit-part players in the opposition. More important are establishment figures – senior politicians, leading officials in international organisations and in NGOs, prominent CEOs, distinguished journalists and academics. They are what David Henderson calls New Millennium Collectivists who push for soft and hard interventions in the world economy. They will be a formidable threat to free trade in decades to come.

Looking ahead: making the case for free trade in the new century

The core political and economic case for free trade, in the service of the trinity of freedom, prosperity and security, is as relevant as ever in the early 21st century. It will be as relevant in the decades ahead. The point is to update and adapt it to keep up with ever-changing realities – not least to meet the emerging global challenges described above. How must it adapt?

Liberalism at home and abroad

The post-1945 case for free trade, based on the Bretton Woods compromise and the post-war theory of commercial policy, is too

---

13   John Stuart Mill, *Autobiography*, Penguin Classics, London, 1989 (1873), p. 179.

narrow and mechanical. Free trade should burst these chains and return to its classical-liberal foundations in Smith and Hume.

As outlined in Chapter 2, the Bretton Woods and GATT settlements combined a partial restoration of nineteenth-century free trade with expanding government intervention at home. Post-war trade theory reflected such 'mixed-systems thinking' by decoupling free trade from laissez-faire. In addition, 'liberalism from above' has prevailed: trade liberalisation has relied on international organisations and inter-governmental negotiations.

Both 'mixed-systems thinking' and 'liberalism from above' were politically expedient after World War II; but, over time, they have entrenched misguided conventional wisdoms. The first is that big-government interventionism at home will not flood across borders and overly damage international commerce. The second is that international institutions deliver trade liberalisation 'from outside', and only through 'concessions' to foreigners in a game of haggling. On both counts, New Millennium Collectivists and even supposedly globalisation-friendly social democrats believe that governments have the knowledge, capacity and honesty to remedy domestic and international market failures. They persistently underestimate government failure, both at home and abroad.

'Mixed-systems thinking' forgets that free trade is part and parcel of free markets; it is but an element of a constitutional whole that includes limited government and laissez-faire at home. Of course, there can be no exact return to mid-Victorian British conditions, especially in conditions of modern democratic politics. But free trade should be *recoupled* to laissez-faire, within a framework of rules enforced by limited – but not minimalist – government.

From Hume and Smith to Hayek, the classical-liberal approach to economic order has been to stress the need for general rules of conduct in a more complex world. As the world becomes more complex in globalisation's wake, it does not follow that government activity should become more complex too. In an ever-extending global market economy, governments simply lack the detailed knowledge to make selective interventions work. In Hayek's words, they are 'constitutionally ignorant'. Ratcheting up the output of detailed regulations is not the answer. On the contrary, *simplicity* is the key. Rather than intervening left, right and centre in the economic *process*, governments should concentrate on regulating the overall economic *order*, i.e. the 'framework conditions' of economic activity.[14] To Michael Oakeshott, this requires governments to be 'umpires' of 'civic associations', not 'estate managers' of 'enterprise associations'.[15] Umpiring consists of setting and enforcing general rules of conduct for the economic order as a whole. Estate-managing, in contrast, caters to a superabundance of rent-seeking interests.

General rules of conduct are simple, transparent, non-discriminatory and *negative*: they tell actors what not to do, but otherwise leave them free to do as they wish. They are generally proscriptive, not prescriptive. Applying equally to all, they exist to protect private property rights and contracts in defence of individual freedom, and as the basis for entrepreneurship and growth. They are intended to *limit* government, not extend its regulatory reach.

---

14   Hayek's views on this are most comprehensively set out in his three volumes of *Law, Legislation and Liberty*, Routledge, London, 1982. The distinction between economic process and economic order comes from Walter Eucken, one of the founders of the Freiburg School of Ordoliberalism. See Sally, *Classical Liberalism and International Economic Order*, op. cit., ch. 6.

15   Michael Oakeshott, *Morality and Politics in Modern Europe: The Harvard Lectures*, Yale University Press, New Haven, CT, 1993, pp. 47–58, 100–110.

Within national jurisdictions, these rules are embodied in private (or commercial) law, the legal underbelly of market society. Domestic private law has its external complements in international private law and in aspects of international public law that govern cross-border commerce, especially the MFN and National Treatment clauses of the GATT. The latter enjoin governments *not* to discriminate in international trade. Their effect is to help defend private property rights against big, discretionary government in international transactions.[16]

In essence, classical liberalism, unlike social democracy, emphasises complementary and joined-up approaches to domestic and international economic order. Limited government and laissez-faire at home underpin limited government and free trade abroad; and domestic rules should be similar to international rules.

What about 'liberalism from above'? My view (as set out in Chapter 6) is that 21st-century free trade should rely less on 20th-century 'liberalism from above' and more on 19th-century 'liberalism from below'. With the latter method, the liberalisation impulse comes from national governments acting unilaterally (or autonomously), and spreads internationally by example (or competitive emulation). Unilateral free trade makes economic sense, since welfare gains come more quickly from a country's own, unconditional import liberalisation than they do from protracted international negotiations. It makes political sense too. Governments have the flexibility to initiate policies and emulate better practice abroad in experimental, trial-and-error fashion,

16   Jan Tumlir, 'National sovereignty, power and interest', *Ordo*, 31, 1980, p. 3; 'International economic order and democratic constitutionalism', op. cit., p. 72; Sally, *Classical Liberalism and International Economic Order*, op. cit., ch. 8.

tailored to specific local conditions. The WTO and bilateral/ regional trade agreements can be helpful auxiliaries in advancing a liberalisation agenda, but they are poor substitutes for unilateral, bottom-up liberalisation.

National governance

National governance is as crucial as ever. This statement contradicts the shibboleths of 'global governance'. Votaries of the latter say that the nation-state is in retreat before the advancing battalions of globalisation. National governments, acting separately and independently, are unable to cope with global problems such as pollution, disease, job losses and health, education and gender issues. The core prescription follows: 'global governance' should provide 'global solutions' to tackle 'global problems'. Global governance should involve partnerships of governments, international organisations, NGOs, big business and organised labour, acting in concert across a wide range of public policies.[17]

This world-view is utterly distorted. In all developed countries, and in most developing countries, national governments, not inter-governmental organisations (IGOs), NGOs or multinational enterprise (MNEs), provide core functions of law and public policy. These functions of national governance – defence of territory from external threat, political stability and internal law and order, the protection of property rights, the provision of macroeconomic stability and other public goods – are as vital as ever. Governments still set the policy stance on international trade, FDI, portfolio capital flows and the cross-border movement

17   For a representative view, see Grunberg et al., op. cit.

of people. National policy, much more than any instrument of global governance, shapes national institutions. It is this combination of national policies and institutions which largely determines national integration with the global economy and national economic performance.[18]

Right through the nineteenth century, national governance, in the context of a decentralised system of nation-states, coexisted with increasing international economic integration. Has the globalisation-and-governance equation changed so much over a century later? Arguably it has not. Globalisation continues to depend fundamentally on law-governed nation-states. To put it another way, the preconditions of a good or bad, healthy or sick, liberal or illiberal international economic order are to be found 'within and beneath', as Wilhelm Röpke put it – in the subsoil of nation-states.

This is not to deny the importance of international cooperation where national-level action is insufficient. Even a sceptic of global governance may concede that there are legitimate zones of international cooperation, and that more of it is required now compared with in the nineteenth century. Good policy demands, however, a clear specification of problems; and, if concerted action is necessary, a sense of the extent and limits of such action. Multilateralism works when it has easy-to-grasp, limited, realistic means and ends. That is an argument for caution and modesty. Unfortunately, the post-1945 record of most international institutions has been one of hubristic ambition, empty rhetoric, diffuse

---

18   There are exceptions to such a generalisation. First, the EU has substantial supranational competence, especially in relations with third countries. But the EU is *sui generis*. Second, failed and failing states do not provide, or hardly provide, the core functions mentioned. These, however, are the exceptions, not the rule.

and mutually contradictory objectives, dysfunctional bureaucracy, and indeed corruption. It has mostly exacerbated misguided government intervention at home. The aid business is a case in point. The GATT was a notable exception; but the same cannot be said of the WTO. To cap it all, the global-governance catchphrase – 'global solutions for global problems' – assumes, wrongly, that most problems have to be dealt with by members of the 'international community'. The latter are usually unaccountable, unrepresentative and distant. It is this unconditional embrace of global governance which is glib, illiberal and dangerous.

Wider geopolitical realities

Trade policy must work with the grain of wider geopolitical realities. This monograph has placed trade policy in the frame of economic policy; and it has stressed the primacy of national economic policies and institutions. But trade policy also links up to foreign policy and international politics, for this frame is also indispensable. A reasonably stable international political order is the categorical imperative for economic development. Without the global pax – an orderly framework for international relations – there can be no security for national and international commerce.

Geopolitical realities have changed since the end of the cold war. No serious challenge exists to US leadership abroad after the collapse of the Soviet imperium. Europe and Japan are internally sclerotic and externally pusillanimous. Long-term demographic trends, with ageing and shrinking populations, make European and Japanese leadership prospects bleaker. Other powers are on the rise, notably China and India. The transatlantic alliance, while still important, is no longer the fulcrum of international relations.

Politics and economics are shifting inexorably in an Asia-Pacific direction. Finally, there are new security challenges, especially after September 11th.

The one constant in this shifting political template is US leadership. For the foreseeable future, the USA will remain the indispensable anchor for global security, prosperity and freedom – far more important than any international organisation or international treaty. It is vital that it leads from the front: in securing the global pax against systemic threats; in dealing with failed states; in maintaining open and stable international financial markets; and, not least, in containing protectionism and encouraging the further liberalisation of trade, capital flows and the movement of people around the world. The USA must also lead by example, setting the standard for liberal economic policies worldwide by what it does at home. This includes untying existing knots of domestic protectionism.

US leadership has to be exercised on several tracks: unilaterally; bilaterally and regionally, especially in relations with other powers; and multilaterally through international institutions. Daunting domestic and external obstacles stand in the way of the enlightened exercise of US power and influence abroad. Domestic politics is shot through with parochialism, protectionism and short-termism, all of which increasingly hamper the exercise of a credible, long-term, outward-looking foreign policy. Externally, the USA has been over-ideological, unempirical and hamfisted in its dealings with other powers and in international institutions, especially under the Bush administration. But robust US leadership is *sine qua non* to constructive relations among major powers, and to the future relevance and workability of international institutions such as the WTO, the IMF and the World Bank. They would be lame and sidelined without it.

More crucial than ever will be US relations with the rising powers of Asia-Pacific, China and India. Here there are welcome trends. Both the Clinton and Bush administrations have pursued 'constructive engagement' with China and India, largely driven by deepening commercial links. But this is frequently thrown off balance by protectionist pressures and foreign-policy hawks who wish to 'contain' rather than 'engage' China in particular. It is vital that these forces are contained so that constructive engagement can continue. This will in turn reinforce positive foreign-policy trends in China and India.

What about foreign policy in China and India? The imperatives of China's modern foreign policy are steady integration into the global economy and political stability in the East Asian neighbourhood. These objectives have driven fundamental change in China's relations with other major powers, and its participation in international institutions. Constructive engagement characterises China's key bilateral relationships and its role in international institutions. Trade diplomacy, multilaterally in the WTO and on bilateral and regional tracks, is perhaps the most visible sign of this foreign-policy transformation.

Set against these very real trends, however, are occasional tendencies of aggressive nationalism. This seems to be directed at Taiwan and Japan, notwithstanding ever-closer commercial ties with them. Finally, the Chinese government seems happy to maintain cosy relations with some of the most repulsive regimes around the world – not least with African governments in the scramble to secure energy supplies. An optimist would argue that foreign policy will ultimately be swayed by the imperatives of global economic integration. Optimism, however, should always be tinged with realism.

India's foreign policy has undergone a parallel transformation since the end of the Cold War. It has switched from leadership of the 'non-aligned' Third World and support for the Soviet Union to constructive engagement with other powers in the developed and developing worlds. Its relations with the USA are blossoming, both on the high politics of security and the low politics of commercial relations. It is playing a more forward-looking, system-maintaining rather than system-wrecking game in international institutions. This has not yet translated, however, into much more pragmatic and flexible diplomacy in the WTO – one key difference with China.

Conclusion

I have argued extensively that the impulse for freer trade does not and will not come from international institutions. Global-governance chatter and blueprints are mere flatulence and fluff. Rather, the liberalisation impulse comes and will come from national governance and unilateral example-setting, especially from Asia and from China in particular. A serviceable multilateralism is important, especially in the WTO. But that can only happen with suitably modest and realistic goals and instruments. Finally, enlightened US leadership and constructive engagement among major powers are the requisites for the preservation of the global pax.

Asia's transformation of the world economy holds out huge opportunities for growth, poverty reduction, improvements in human welfare, and for the extension of economic freedom. Not least, it will contribute to peaceful international relations as nations and peoples come closer together through commercial ties. For the first time in world history, it is Asia, not the West, which represents the best hope for the free-trade trinity of prosperity, freedom and peace. That has profound political and economic ramifications.

More generally, liberal optimists would conclude that global prospects today look a lot better than they did a century ago. Interstate political and military rivalry today is low-grade compared with pre-World War I jingoism. Post-1945 globalisation has created powerful commercial interests with strong stakes in open markets. New Millennium Collectivism is not as noxious as the deadly ideological combination of nationalism and socialism in the first half of the twentieth century.[19]

But nothing is pre-programmed – that is the eternal lesson of summer 1914. The magnitude of unfolding changes in the global economy is bound to increase protectionist pressures, in developed and developing countries. Governments, not least in China and India, have to manage internal problems such as rising regional disparities, rotting public sectors, environmental pollution, corruption, and anxiety about health, education and pensions systems among the most vulnerable. Then there is the problematic link between a spreading market economy and authoritarian politics, particularly in China. Finally, there are international security flashpoints, such as relationships between China and Taiwan and China and Japan, China's growing military power in East Asia, and the big-power scramble for global energy supplies – not to mention Islamic fundamentalism, international terrorism, rogue states and failed states. All these could slow down or even halt the onward march of global economic integration.

---

19   Wolf, *Why Globalisation Works*, op. cit., pp. 308–13.

Good management of international economic policy requires what Martin Wolf calls 'liberal realism'. This involves a balance between power politics and cooperation in international institutions; working with the grain of outward-looking commercial interests (such as exporters, downstream users of imported inputs, multinational firms with global production networks, cities and regions seeking to attract FDI) that can counter inward-looking protectionist interests; and taking advantage of (often unanticipated) events.

Ideas also have their place in this scheme; and they are not to be underestimated. That is why I have made the case for free trade in a classical-liberal, limited-government, laissez-faire framework – and not as part of a social democracy I find mealy mouthed, internally contradictory and not well fitted for 21st-century globalisation. The idea of free trade now lacks the commanding champions it once had – the likes of mid-Victorian titans such as Peel, Gladstone, Cobden and Bright, or 20th-century equivalents such as Cordell Hull and Ludwig Erhard. To repeat John Stuart Mill's felicitous words: it is 'the word in season, which, at a critical moment, does much to decide the result.' Thus it falls to free trade's friends to spread their word *in season with* the global political and economic currents of the new century.

REFERENCES

Antkiewicz, A. and J. Whalley (2005), 'China's new regional trade agreements', *World Economy*, 28(10): 1539–56.

Athukorala, P. (2006), 'Product fragmentation and trade patterns in east Asia', *Asian Economic Papers*, 4(3): 1–27.

Axelrod, R. and R. O. Keohane (1993), 'Achieving co-operation under anarchy', in D. Baldwin (ed.), *Neorealism and Neoliberalism: The Contemporary Debate*, New York: Columbia University Press.

Balcerowicz, L. (1995), *Socialism, Capitalism, Transformation*, Budapest: Central European University Press.

Baldwin, R. (2006a), 'Implications of European experiences with regionalism for future economic integration in Asia', Mimeo.

Baldwin, R. (2006b), 'Multilateralising regionalism: spaghetti bowls as building blocs on the path to global free trade', *World Economy*, 29(11): 1451–1518.

Barfield, C. (2001), *Free Trade, Sovereignty, Democracy: The Future of the World Trade Organisation*, Washington, DC: American Enterprise Institute.

Bauer, P. T. (2000a), 'Foreign aid: abiding issues', in P. T. Bauer (ed.), *From Subsistence to Exchange and Other Essays*, Princeton, NJ: Princeton University Press.

Bauer, P. T. (2000b), 'Western guilt and Third World poverty', in P. T. Bauer (ed.), *From Subsistence to Exchange and Other Essays*, Princeton, NJ: Princeton University Press.

Beattie, A. (2007), 'Avoiding the crush', *Financial Times*, 14 June.

Bergsten, C. F. (2007), 'Toward a Free Trade Area of the Asia Pacific', Policy Briefs in International Economics no. PB07–2, Peterson Institute for International Economics, www.petersoninstitute.org.

Bhagwati, J. (2002), *Free Trade Today*, Princeton, NJ: Princeton University Press.

Bhagwati, J. and T. N. Srinivasan (1999), 'Outward-orientation and development: are revisionists right?', Yale University Economic Growth Centre Discussion Paper no. 806.

Bhattasali, D., L. Shantong and W. Martin (2004), *China's Accession to the World Trade Organization, Policy Reform and Poverty Reduction*, Washington, DC: World Bank.

Chang, H. J. (2002), *Kicking Away the Ladder: Development Strategy in Historical Perspective*, London: Anthem Press.

Collier, P. (2007), *The Bottom Billion*, Oxford: Oxford University Press.

Crawford, J. A. and R. V. Fiorentino (2005), 'The changing landscape of regional trade agreements', WTO Discussion Paper no. 8, www.wto.org.

Dean, J. (1995), 'The trade-policy revolution in developing countries', *The World Economy, Global Trade Policy Review 1995*, Autumn, Vol. 18, Issue 5, pp. 173–90. Reprinted in: C. Milner, ed., *Developing and Newly Industrializing Countries*, Cheltenham: Edward Elgar, 1998.

Drabek, Z. and S. Laird (1998), 'The New Liberalism: trade-policy developments in emerging markets', *Journal of World Trade*, 32(5): 241–69.

Easterly, W. (2006), *The White Man's Burden: Why the West's Efforts to Aid the Rest Have Done So Much Ill and So Little Good*, New York: Penguin.

Economist (2006), 'The new titans', *The Economist* Survey of the World Economy, 14 September.

Erixon, F. and R. Sally (2006), 'Trade and aid: countering New Millennium Collectivism', *Australian Economic Review*, 39(1): 69–77.

Estevadeordal, A. and K. Suominen (2003), 'Rules of origin in the world trading system', Paper prepared for the seminar on regional trade agreements and the WTO, World Trade Organization, Washington, DC, 14 November, www.wto.org.

Esty, D. (2002), 'The World Trade Organization's legitimacy crisis', *World Trade Review*, 1(1): 7–22.

Evenett, S. (ed.) (2006), 'The European Union's new trade policy', Special Issue, *Aussenwirtschaft*, 61(IV).

Evenett, S. (2007), 'EU commercial policy in a multipolar trading system', Mimeo.

Frieden, J. and R. Rogowski (1996), 'The impact of the international economy on national policies', in R. Keohane and H. Milner (eds), *Internationalisation and Domestic Politics*, Cambridge: Cambridge University Press.

Goldstein, J. (1994), *Ideas, Interests and American Trade Policy*, Ithaca, NY: Cornell University Press.

Grunberg, I., I. Kaul and M. Stern (eds) (1999), *Global Public Goods: International Co-operation in the 21st Century*, New York and Oxford: Oxford University Press.

Haggard, S. and J. Williamson (1993), 'The political conditions for economic reform', in J. Williamson (ed.), *The Political Economy of Policy Reform*, Washington, DC, Institute for International Economics, pp. 527–96.

Hayek, F. A. (1944), *The Road to Serfdom*, London: Routledge.

Hayek, F. A. (1982), *Law, Legislation and Liberty*, London: Routledge.

Henderson, D. (1992), 'International economic integration: progress, prospects and implications', *International Affairs*, 64(4): 633–53.

Henderson, D. (1998), *The Changing Fortunes of Economic Liberalism: Yesterday, Today and Tomorrow*, London: Institute of Economic Affairs.

Henderson, D. (2001), *Anti-Liberalism 2000: The Rise of New Millennium Collectivism*, London: Institute of Economic Affairs.

Henderson, D. (2004a), *Misguided Virtue: False Notions of Corporate Social Responsibility*, London: Institute of Economic Affairs.

Henderson, D. (2004b), 'Globalisation, economic progress and New Millennium Collectivism', *World Economics*, 5(3): 43–73.

Howe, A. (1997), *Free Trade and Liberal England, 1846–1946*, Oxford: Clarendon Press.

Hull, C. (1948), 'The true nature of trade', in *The Memoirs of Cordell Hull*, New York: Macmillan.

Hume, D. (1970) [1758], 'Of the jealousy of trade', in E. Rotwein (ed.), *Writings on Economics*, Madison: University of Wisconsin Press.

Ianchovichina, E. and W. Martin (2001), 'Trade liberalisation in China's accession to the World Trade Organization', World

Bank Policy Research Working Paper 2623,
www.worldbank.org.

Ingco, M. D. and J. D. Nash (eds) (2004), *Agriculture and the WTO: Creating a Trading System for Development*, Washington, DC: World Bank.

Irwin, D. A. (1996), *Against the Tide: An Intellectual History of Free Trade*, Princeton, NJ: Princeton University Press.

Keohane, R. O. (1984), *After Hegemony: Co-operation and Discord in the World Political Economy*, Princeton, NJ: Princeton University Press.

Keohane, R. O. (1986), 'Reciprocity in international relations', *International Organisation*, 40(1): 1–27.

Kravis, I. (1970), 'Trade as a handmaiden of growth: similarities between the nineteenth and twentieth centuries', *Economic Journal*, LXXX: 850–72.

Krueger, A. O. (1974), 'The political economy of the rent-seeking society', *American Economic Review*, 64(3): 291–303.

Kuczynski, P. P. and J. Williamson (eds) (2004), *After the Washington Consensus: Restarting Growth and Reform in Latin America*, Washington, DC: Institute for International Economics.

Lal, D. (1998), *Unintended Consequences: The Impact of Factor Endowments, Culture and Politics on Long-Run Economic Performance*, Cambridge, MA: MIT Press.

Lal, D. (2006), *Reviving the Invisible Hand: The Case for Classical Liberalism in the Twenty-first Century*, Princeton, NJ: Princeton University Press.

Lal, D. and H. Myint (1996), *The Political Economy of Poverty, Equity and Growth: A Comparative Study*, Oxford: Clarendon Press.

Lardy, N. (2002), *Integrating China into the Global Economy*, Washington, DC: Brookings Institution.

Legrain, P. (2006), *Immigrants: Your Country Needs Them*, London: Little, Brown.

Lindsey, B. (2002), *Against the Dead Hand: The Uncertain Struggle for Global Capitalism*, Washington, DC: John Wiley.

Little, I. M. D. (1999), 'Trade and industrialisation revisited', in I. M. D. Little, *Collection and Recollections*, Oxford: Clarendon Press.

Maddison, A. (2003), *The World Economy: Historical Statistics*, Paris: OECD.

Mattoo, A. (2003), 'China's accession to the WTO: the services dimension', *Journal of International Economic Law*, 6(2): 299–339.

Mattoo, A. and R. Stern (eds) (2003), *India and the WTO*, Washington, DC: World Bank/OUP.

Messerlin, P. (2006), *Europe After the 'No' Votes: Mapping a New Economic Path*, London: Institute of Economic Affairs.

Michalopoulos, C. (2001), *Developing Countries and the WTO*, London: Palgrave.

Mill, J. S. (1989) [1873], *Autobiography*, London: Penguin Classics.

Myint, H. (1958), 'The "classical theory" of international trade and the underdeveloped countries', *Economic Journal*, LXVIII(270), June: 317–337.

Myint, H. (1977), 'Adam Smith's theory of international trade in the perspective of economic development', *Economica*, 44 (3): 231–248.

Myrdal, G. (1968), *Asian Drama: An Inquiry into the Poverty of Nations*, 3 vols, Harmondsworth: Penguin.

Oakeshott, M. (1993), *Morality and Politics in Modern Europe: The Harvard Lectures*, New Haven, CT: Yale University Press.

OECD (2007), *Economic Policy Reforms: Going for Growth*, Paris: OECD.

Olson, M. (1971), *The Logic of Collective Action: Public Goods and the Theory of Groups*, Cambridge, MA: Harvard University Press.

Olson, M. (1982), *The Rise and Decline of Nations: Economic Growth, Stagflation and Social Rigidities*, New Haven, CT: Yale University Press.

Orwell, G. (1984), *Nineteen Eighty-Four*, in G. Orwell, *The Complete Novels*, London: Penguin.

Oxfam (2002), *Rigged Rules and Double Standards: Trade, Globalisation and the Fight Against Poverty*, Oxford: Oxfam International, www.marketradefair.com.

Robbins, L. (1936), *Economic Planning and International Order*, London: Macmillan.

Robbins, L. (1958), *Robert Torrens and the Evolution of Classical Economics*, London: Macmillan.

Robbins, L. (1998), *A History of Economic Thought: The LSE Lectures*, ed. S. Medema and W. Samuels, Princeton, NJ: Princeton University Press.

Rodrik, D. (1998), *The New Global Economy and Developing Countries: Making Openness Work*, Washington, DC: Overseas Development Council.

Rodrik, D. (2001), 'Trading in illusions', *Foreign Policy*, March/April, www.foreignpolicy.com/issue_marapr_2001/rodrick.html.

Rogowski, R. (1990), *Commerce and Coalitions: How Trade Affects Domestic Political Alignments*, Princeton, NJ: Princeton University Press.

Röpke, W. (1959), *International Order and Economic Integration*, Dordrecht: Reidel.

Sachs, J. (2005), *The End of Poverty: How We Can Make it Happen in Our Lifetime*, London: Penguin.

Sachs, J. and A. Warner (1995), 'Economic reform and the process of global integration', Brookings Papers on Economic Activity no. 1.

Sally, R. (1998), *Classical Liberalism and International Economic Order: Studies in Theory and Intellectual History*, London: Routledge.

Sally, R. (2006a), 'Chinese trade policies in wider Asian perspective', in Y. Yao and L. Yueh (eds), *Globalisation and Economic Growth in China*, London: World Scientific Publishing.

Sally, R. (2006b), 'FTAs and the prospects for regional integration in Asia', ECIPE Working Paper 1, www.ecipe.org/publications/2006/WPno1_06_Sally.pdf.

Sally, R. (2007), 'Trade policy in Asia', ECIPE Policy Brief no.1, www.ecipe.org/pdf/Policybrief_0107.pdf.

Sally, R. and R. Sen (2005), 'Whither trade policies in southeast Asia? The wider Asian and global context', *ASEAN Economic Bulletin*, 22(1): 92–115.

Schumpeter, J. A. (1950), *History of Economic Analysis*, London: Routledge.

Seabright, P. (2004), *The Company of Strangers*, Princeton, NJ: Princeton University Press.

Sen, R. (2006), '"New Regionalism" in Asia: a comparative analysis of emerging regional and bilateral trading agreements involving ASEAN, China and India', *Journal of World Trade*, 40(4): 553–96.

Smith, A. (1976) [1776], *An Inquiry into the Nature and Causes of the Wealth of Nations*, ed. E. Cannan, Chicago, IL: University of Chicago Press.

Soesastro, H. (2006), 'Regional integration in east Asia: achievements and future prospects', *Asian Economic Policy Review*, 1(2): 215–34.

Stiglitz, J. (2002), *Globalisation and Its Discontents*, London: Allen Lane.

Summers, L. (2006a), 'Lack of fear gives cause for concern', *Financial Times*, 26 December.

Summers, L. (2006b), 'The global middle class cries out for reassurance', *Financial Times*, 29 October.

Summers, L. (2007), 'Harnessing market forces to share prosperity', *Financial Times*, 24 June.

Sutherland, P. et al. (2005), *The Future of the WTO: Addressing Institutional Challenges in the New Millennium*, Geneva: WTO.

Tumlir, J. (1980), 'National sovereignty, power and interest', *Ordo*, 31: 1–26.

Tumlir, J. (1983a), 'International economic order and democratic constitutionalism', *Ordo*, 34: 71–83.

Tumlir, J. (1983b), 'Need for an open multilateral trading system', *World Economy*, 6(4): 393–408.

UN Millennium Project (2005), *Investing in Development: A Practical Plan to Achieve the Millennium Development Goals*, New York: Earthscan.

Viner, J. (1937), *Studies in the Theory of International Trade*, London: Allen and Unwin.

Viner, J. (1991), *Essays on the Intellectual History of Economics*, ed. D. A. Irwin, Princeton, NJ: Princeton University Press.

Williamson, J. (ed.) (1993), *The Political Economy of Policy Reform*, Washington, DC: Institute for International Economics.

Winters, A. L. (2004a), 'Trade liberalisation and economic performance: an overview', *Economic Journal*, 114, February, pp. F4–F21.

Winters, A. L. (2004b), 'Trade liberalisation and poverty', *Journal of Economic Literature*, 42(1).

Wolf, M. (2003), 'Why Europe was the past, the US is the present and a China-dominated Asia the future of the global economy', *Financial Times*, 22 September.

Wolf, M. (2004a), 'Three reasons to be cheerful about the world economy', *Financial Times*, 30 June.

Wolf, M. (2004b), *Why Globalisation Works: The Case for the Global Market Economy*, New Haven, CT: Yale University Press.

Wolf, M. (2005), 'On the move: Asia's giants take different routes in pursuit of economic greatness', *Financial Times*, 23 February.

Wolf, M. (2006a), 'A new gilded age', *Financial Times*, 25 April.

Wolf, M. (2006b), 'Answer to Asia's rise is not to retreat', *Financial Times*, 14 March.

Wolf, M. (2006c), 'China should stick to trial and error – but risk bolder trials', *Financial Times*, 7 June.

Wolf, M. (2006d), 'Confronting seismic economic shifts', *Financial Times*, 31 January.

Wolf, M. (2006e), 'What India must do to outpace China', *Financial Times*, 14 February.

Wolf, M. (2007), 'A divided world of economic success and political turmoil', *Financial Times*, 30 January.

World Bank (1993), *The East Asian Miracle*, Washington, DC: World Bank.

World Bank (1998a), *1998 Annual Review of Development Effectiveness*, World Bank Operations Evaluation Department, Washington, DC: World Bank.

World Bank (1998b), *Assessing Aid: What Works, What Doesn't, and Why*, Oxford: Oxford University Press.

World Bank (2002), *Globalisation, Growth and Poverty: Building an Inclusive World Economy*, Washington, DC: World Bank.

World Bank (2004), *Global Economic Prospects 2005: Trade, Regionalism and Development*, Washington, DC: World Bank/ OUP.

World Bank (2005), 'Regional trade agreements and development: upside potential and downside risks', Trade Note 24, 13 September, www.worldbank.org.

World Bank (2006), *Doing Business in 2007*, Washington, DC: World Bank.

World Bank governance indicators, www.worldbank.org.

WTO (World Trade Organization) (2000), *Report of the Working Party on the Accession of China*, the *Draft Protocol on the Accession of the People's Republic of China*, and attached Annexes with schedules of concessions on goods and services, all in WT/MIN(01)/3, www.wto.org.

WTO (2001a), *Declaration on the TRIPS Agreement and Public Health*, WT/MIN(01)/DEC/W/2, 14 November, www.wto. org.

WTO (2001b), *Implementation-related Issues and Concerns*, WT/MIN(01)/W/10, 14 November, www.wto.org.

WTO (2001c), *Ministerial Declaration*, WT/MIN(01)/DEC/W/1, 14 November, www.wto.org.

WTO (2002), *Rules-of-origin Regimes in Regional Trade Agreements*, Background survey by the Secretariat, Committee on Regional Trade Agreements, WT/REG/W/45, 5 April, www.wto.org.

WTO (2005), *Ministerial Declaration* and *Ministerial Declaration: Annexes*, WT/MIN(05)/DEC, 18 December, www.wto.org/english/thewto_e/minist_e/min05_e/final_text_e.htm.

WTO (2006), *International Trade Statistics 2005*, Geneva: WTO.

WTO (2007a), *Trade Policy Review: India 2007*, WT/TPR/S/182, 18 April, Geneva: WTO, www.wto.org/english/tratop_e/trp_e/s182–00_e.doc.

WTO (2007b), *Regional Trade Agreements: Facts and Figures*, www.wto.org/english/tratop_e/region_e/regfac_e.htm.

Zakaria, F. (2003), *The Future of Democracy: Illiberal Democracy at Home and Abroad*, New York: W. W. Norton.

Zoellick, R. (2005), 'Whither China: from membership to responsibility?', Speech on US–China Relations and Remarks to the National Committee on US–China Relations, New York City, September, www.state.gov/s/d/rem/53682.htm.

INDEX

ABOUT THE IEA

The Institute is a research and educational charity (No. CC 235 351), limited by guarantee. Its mission is to improve understanding of the fundamental institutions of a free society by analysing and expounding the role of markets in solving economic and social problems.

The IEA achieves its mission by:

- a high-quality publishing programme
- conferences, seminars, lectures and other events
- outreach to school and college students
- brokering media introductions and appearances

The IEA, which was established in 1955 by the late Sir Antony Fisher, is an educational charity, not a political organisation. It is independent of any political party or group and does not carry on activities intended to affect support for any political party or candidate in any election or referendum, or at any other time. It is financed by sales of publications, conference fees and voluntary donations.

In addition to its main series of publications the IEA also publishes a quarterly journal, *Economic Affairs*.

The IEA is aided in its work by a distinguished international Academic Advisory Council and an eminent panel of Honorary Fellows. Together with other academics, they review prospective IEA publications, their comments being passed on anonymously to authors. All IEA papers are therefore subject to the same rigorous independent refereeing process as used by leading academic journals.

IEA publications enjoy widespread classroom use and course adoptions in schools and universities. They are also sold throughout the world and often translated/reprinted.

Since 1974 the IEA has helped to create a worldwide network of 100 similar institutions in over 70 countries. They are all independent but share the IEA's mission.

Views expressed in the IEA's publications are those of the authors, not those of the Institute (which has no corporate view), its Managing Trustees, Academic Advisory Council members or senior staff.

Members of the Institute's Academic Advisory Council, Honorary Fellows, Trustees and Staff are listed on the following page.

The Institute gratefully acknowledges financial support for its publications programme and other work from a generous benefaction by the late Alec and Beryl Warren.

The Institute of Economic Affairs
2 Lord North Street, Westminster, London SW1P 3LB
Tel: 020 7799 8900
Fax: 020 7799 2137
Email: iea@iea.org.uk
Internet: iea.org.uk

Other papers recently published by the IEA include:

The Changing Fortunes of Economic Liberalism
Yesterday, Today and Tomorrow
David Henderson
Occasional Paper 105 (new edition); ISBN 0 255 36520 9; £12.50

The Global Education Industry
Lessons from Private Education in Developing Countries
James Tooley
Hobart Paper 141 (new edition); ISBN 0 255 36503 9; £12.50

Saving Our Streams
The Role of the Anglers' Conservation Association in
Protecting English and Welsh Rivers
Roger Bate
Research Monograph 53; ISBN 0 255 36494 6; £10.00

Better Off Out?
The Benefits or Costs of EU Membership
Brian Hindley & Martin Howe
Occasional Paper 99 (new edition); ISBN 0 255 36502 0; £10.00

Buckingham at 25
Freeing the Universities from State Control
Edited by James Tooley
Readings 55; ISBN 0 255 36512 8; £15.00

Lectures on Regulatory and Competition Policy
Irwin M. Stelzer
Occasional Paper 120; ISBN 0 255 36511 x; £12.50

Misguided Virtue
False Notions of Corporate Social Responsibility
David Henderson
Hobart Paper 142; ISBN 0 255 36510 1; £12.50

HIV and Aids in Schools
The Political Economy of Pressure Groups and Miseducation
Barrie Craven, Pauline Dixon, Gordon Stewart & James Tooley
Occasional Paper 121; ISBN 0 255 36522 5; £10.00

The Road to Serfdom
The Reader's Digest *condensed version*
Friedrich A. Hayek
Occasional Paper 122; ISBN 0 255 36530 6; £7.50

Bastiat's *The Law*
Introduction by Norman Barry
Occasional Paper 123; ISBN 0 255 36509 8; £7.50

A Globalist Manifesto for Public Policy
Charles Calomiris
Occasional Paper 124; ISBN 0 255 36525 X; £7.50

Euthanasia for Death Duties
Putting Inheritance Tax Out of Its Misery
Barry Bracewell-Milnes
Research Monograph 54; ISBN 0 255 36513 6; £10.00

Liberating the Land
The Case for Private Land-use Planning
Mark Pennington
Hobart Paper 143; ISBN 0 255 36508 X; £10.00

IEA Yearbook of Government Performance 2002/2003
Edited by Peter Warburton
Yearbook 1; ISBN 0 255 36532 2; £15.00

Britain's Relative Economic Performance, 1870–1999
Nicholas Crafts
Research Monograph 55; ISBN 0 255 36524 1; £10.00

Economy and Virtue
Essays on the Theme of Markets and Morality
Edited by Dennis O'Keeffe
Readings 59; ISBN 0 255 36504 7; £12.50

Free Markets Under Siege
Cartels, Politics and Social Welfare
Richard A. Epstein
Occasional Paper 132; ISBN 0 255 36553 5; £10.00

Unshackling Accountants
D. R. Myddelton
Hobart Paper 149; ISBN 0 255 36559 4; £12.50

The Euro as Politics
Pedro Schwartz
Research Monograph 58; ISBN 0 255 36535 7; £12.50

Pricing Our Roads
Vision and Reality
Stephen Glaister & Daniel J. Graham
Research Monograph 59; ISBN 0 255 36562 4; £10.00

The Role of Business in the Modern World
Progress, Pressures, and Prospects for the Market Economy
David Henderson
Hobart Paper 150; ISBN 0 255 36548 9; £12.50

Public Service Broadcasting Without the BBC?
Alan Peacock
Occasional Paper 133; ISBN 0 255 36565 9; £10.00

The ECB and the Euro: the First Five Years
Otmar Issing
Occasional Paper 134; ISBN 0 255 36555 1; £10.00

Wheels of Fortune
Self-funding Infrastructure and the Free Market Case for a Land Tax
Fred Harrison
Hobart Paper 154; ISBN 0 255 36589 6; £12.50

Were 364 Economists All Wrong?
Edited by Philip Booth
Readings 60; ISBN 978 0 255 36588 8; £10.00

Europe After the 'No' Votes
Mapping a New Economic Path
Patrick A. Messerlin
Occasional Paper 139; ISBN 978 0 255 36580 2; £10.00

The Railways, the Market and the Government
John Hibbs et al.
Readings 61; ISBN 978 0 255 36567 3; £12.50

Corruption: The World's Big C
Cases, Causes, Consequences, Cures
Ian Senior
Research Monograph 61; ISBN 978 0 255 36571 0; £12.50

Choice and the End of Social Housing
Peter King
Hobart Paper 155; ISBN 978 0 255 36568 0; £10.00

Sir Humphrey's Legacy
Facing Up to the Cost of Public Sector Pensions
Neil Record
Hobart Paper 156; ISBN 978 0 255 36578 9; £10.00

The Economics of Law
Cento Veljanovski
Second edition
Hobart Paper 157; ISBN 978 0 255 36561 1; £12.50

Living with Leviathan
Public Spending, Taxes and Economic Performance
David B. Smith
Hobart Paper 158; ISBN 978 0 255 36579 6; £12.50

The Vote Motive
Gordon Tullock
New edition
Hobart Paperback 33; ISBN 978 0 255 36577 2; £10.00

Waging the War of Ideas
John Blundell
Third edition
Occasional Paper 131; ISBN 978 0 255 36606 9; £12.50

The War Between the State and the Family
How Government Divides and Impoverishes
Patricia Morgan
Hobart Paper 159; ISBN 978 0 255 36596 3; £10.00

Capitalism – A Condensed Version
Arthur Seldon
Occasional Paper 140; ISBN 978 0 255 36598 7; £7.50

Catholic Social Teaching and the Market Economy
Edited by Philip Booth
Hobart Paperback 34; ISBN 978 0 255 36581 9; £15.00

Adam Smith – A Primer
Eamonn Butler
Occasional Paper 141; ISBN 978 0 255 36608 3; £7.50

Happiness, Economics and Public Policy
Helen Johns & Paul Ormerod
Research Monograph 62; ISBN 978 0 255 36600 7; £10.00

They Meant Well
Government Project Disasters
D. R. Myddelton
Hobart Paper 160; ISBN 978 0 255 36601 4; £12.50

Rescuing Social Capital from Social Democracy
John Meadowcroft & Mark Pennington
Hobart Paper 161; ISBN 978 0 255 36592 5; £10.00

Paths to Property
Approaches to Institutional Change in International Development
Karol Boudreaux & Paul Dragos Aligica
Hobart Paper 162; ISBN 978 0 255 36582 6; £10.00

Prohibitions
Edited by John Meadowcroft
Hobart Paperback 35; ISBN 978 0 255 36585 7; £15.00

Sixty Years On – Who Cares for the NHS?
Helen Evans
Research Monograph 63; ISBN 978 0 255 36611 3; £10.00

Taming Leviathan
Waging the War of Ideas Around the World
Edited by Colleen Dyble
Occasional Paper 142; ISBN 978 0 255 36607 6; £12.50

The Legal Foundations of Free Markets
Edited by Stephen F. Copp
Hobart Paperback 36; ISBN 978 0 255 36591 8; £15.00

Climate Change Policy: Challenging the Activists
Edited by Colin Robinson
Readings 62; ISBN 978 0 255 36595 6; £10.00

Should We Mind the Gap?
Gender Pay Differentials and Public Policy
J. R. Shackleton
Hobart Paper 164; ISBN 978 0 255 36604 5; £10.00

Pension Provision: Government Failure Around the World
Edited by Philip Booth et al.
Readings 63; ISBN 978 0 255 36602 1; £15.00

New Europe's Old Regions
Piotr Zientara
Hobart Paper 165; ISBN 978 0 255 36617 5; £12.50

Central Banking in a Free Society
Tim Congdon
Hobart Paper 166; ISBN 978 0 255 36623 6; £12.50

Verdict on the Crash: Causes and Policy Implications
Edited by Philip Booth
Hobart Paperback 37; ISBN 978 0 255 36635 9; £12.50

The European Institutions as an Interest Group
The Dynamics of Ever-Closer Union
Roland Vaubel
Hobart Paper 167; ISBN 978 0 255 36634 2; £10.00

An Adult Approach to Further Education
Alison Wolf
Hobart Paper 168; ISBN 978 0 255 36586 4; £10.00

Other IEA publications

Comprehensive information on other publications and the wider work of the IEA can be found at www.iea.org.uk. To order any publication please see below.

Personal customers

Orders from personal customers should be directed to the IEA:
Bob Layson
IEA
2 Lord North Street
FREEPOST LON10168
London SW1P 3YZ
Tel: 020 7799 8909. Fax: 020 7799 2137
Email: blayson@iea.org.uk

Trade customers

All orders from the book trade should be directed to the IEA's distributor:
Gazelle Book Services Ltd (IEA Orders)
FREEPOST RLYS-EAHU-YSCZ
White Cross Mills
Hightown
Lancaster LA1 4XS
Tel: 01524 68765, Fax: 01524 53232
Email: sales@gazellebooks.co.uk

IEA subscriptions

The IEA also offers a subscription service to its publications. For a single annual payment (currently £42.00 in the UK), subscribers receive every monograph the IEA publishes. For more information please contact:
Adam Myers
Subscriptions
IEA
2 Lord North Street
FREEPOST LON10168
London SW1P 3YZ
Tel: 020 7799 8920, Fax: 020 7799 2137
Email: amyers@iea.org.uk